MARCO POLO

This edition published 2019
by Living Book Press

Images by Witold Gordon from The Travels of Marco Polo (The Venetian), 1926

ISBN: 978-1-925729-52-8 (softcover)
978-1-922348-89-0 (hardcover)
978-1-925729-91-7 (ebook)

A catalogue record for this book is available from the National Library of Australia

Marco Polo

MANUEL KOMROFF

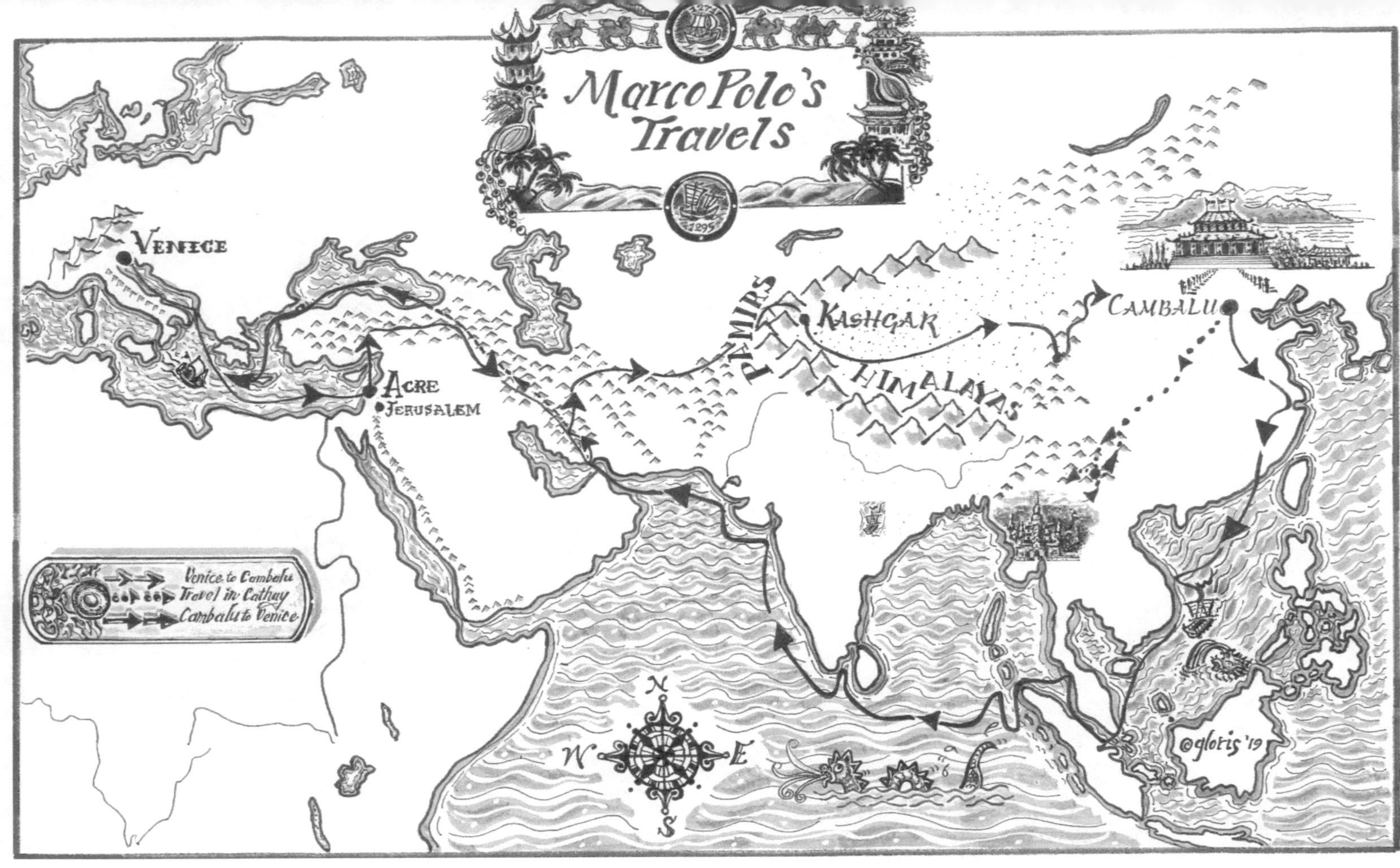

Marco Polo's Travels
1271
1295
Venice
Acre
Jerusalem
Pamirs
Kashgar
Himalayas
Cambalu
Venice to Cambalu
Travel in Cathay
Cambalu to Venice
N
S
W
E
©gloris '19

CONTENTS

CHAPTER I

A BOY IN VENICE

YOUNG MARCO POLO looked out upon the wide blue sea from an upper window in his home in Venice. Far beyond the Gulf of Venice he saw the broad Adriatic dotted with many vessels laden with cargo. And, now and then, he saw one of the war galleys, manned by a hundred oars, racing swiftly over the water to protect the harbour from enemies and the rich cargo vessels from raiders.

And as he looked out upon the blue sea young Marco dreamed. He dreamed of the day when he would set sail for distant ports in Sicily and Greece. He dreamed of visiting the great city of Constantinople where his father and uncle owned buildings and docks. He dreamed of the mysterious lands to which the Crusaders had gone. He, too, might some day visit these far-off places. He, too, might some day see the great wonders of the world.

Entranced he gazed upon the sea, dreaming of the great world that lay beyond. All his life he had lived in the city of Venice. But to this great port vessels arrived from many places and he had heard tales of the lands beyond. He had even heard tales of a world still unknown, a world filled with mysteries and marvels.

There were some who believed that beyond the barrier of the Caucasus there lay vast lands that stretched on and on. And it was said that no one had ever ventured into this unknown world to the east, for the way was barred by the Tartar hordes.

Young Marco wondered if perhaps it was into this unknown

world that his father and uncle had gone. For such a trip, he felt, would take many years. And had not his father and uncle been gone a long time? Much too long. Surely soon, any day, they must return. And he hoped that one of the vessels that he could see entering the harbour of Venice was bringing them home. With all his heart he wished for their return.

Marco was six years old when his father Nicolo and his uncle Maffeo, who was unmarried, sailed out of the port of Venice with a valuable shipload of merchandise. They expected to be gone only a year or two and left young Marco in the care of his grandparents, for his mother had died when he was an infant. But after many years had passed and the Polos did not return, the grandparents feared that Nicolo and Maffeo were lost. Marco, however, never gave up hope. He felt certain that some day his father and uncle would return. He was six when his father and uncle left; now he was fifteen. When they left he was a little boy. Now he felt himself strong and grown.

And one day, during Marco's fifteenth year, just as he had long wished, a vessel entering the harbour of Venice brought back his father and uncle. They had been gone nine long years and now, at last, they were returned to their home.

That evening a banquet was given in the Polo home to welcome back to Venice the two brothers who had travelled far and been away so long. At this feast were many Venetian noblemen, old family friends and relatives, as well as masters from the merchants' guild. Young Marco sat proudly beside his father.

When the feast was done and the table cleared, Marco's father and uncle drew out a large chart which they unrolled on the table for all to see.

"This will help us explain our long journey," said Nicolo. "With this map which we ourselves have drawn, we will try to trace our route and tell you how it happened that we finally arrived at the lands of the Tartars."

At this the guests at the table looked anxiously at each other. There was fear in their eyes, for all knew that the Tartars were a fierce and warlike race. Only fifty years before their armies had reached the Danube. And even at that very moment the terrible Tartars were still a threat to the peace of Europe. How many lands had they already overrun! Would their conquests never end!

"Yes," repeated Nicolo boldly. "We have been to the land of the Tartars."

"It is true," added his brother Maffeo. "We have not only been to the land of the Tartars, but we have seen their emperor Kublai Khan and are now returned as his personal envoys."

The fear in the eyes of the guests now turned to astonishment. All were silent. All were eager to hear what Nicolo and Maffeo were about to relate.

With his finger on the chart Nicolo traced the course of their sailing vessel. "Nine years ago, in the year 1260," he said, "we sailed from the Gulf of Venice." Then he told how, arriving safely at Constantinople, they found their ships and warehouses filled with rich and varied merchandise. Everything was in good order and, since their presence in Constantinople was not urgently required, they decided to investigate the trade possibilities of some of the lands about the Black Sea. In order to do this they were required to travel on horseback. They took with them many costly jewels which they could conceal and carry easily. With these jewels they intended to trade.

After travelling on horseback along the shores of the Black Sea they reached the encampment of one of the Tartar generals. This chief was a liberal prince—one who had respect for culture—and he at once welcomed the Polo brothers and received them with all the honours granted to ambassadors. The Polo brothers remained a whole year as guests of the Tartar Prince. During this time they learnt to speak the Mongolian tongue of the Tartars.

But they found the countries through which they had to pass at war with each other, and because of this they were forced to make a long detour. This detour carried them eastward. They crossed the

Volga River and then spent a full seventeen days travelling through a desolate stretch of desert land. After this they entered the dominions of Persia.

This long route Marco's father Nicolo traced on the map before them. Then pointing to a certain spot he explained that this was the place in Persia where they chanced to meet a distinguished ambassador. This ambassador was on his way to the great Khan of the Tartars who lived in Far Eastern lands.

The ambassador was much impressed with the Polo brothers. He found them cultured and agreeable. They were able to speak together in the Mongolian tongue, and soon the ambassador proposed that the Polo brothers accompany him to the court of Kublai Khan. He was certain that the brothers would be fascinated by the wonders of this land which he called Cathay. And he felt sure that since the Khan had never seen any natives of Europe he would be pleased to welcome them to his court. All this Nicolo explained to his guests seated about the table. Now, with his finger he carefully traced their long journey to the court of the Khan Kublai in far-off Cathay.

"From Persia we travelled in an easterly direction. We travelled many roads and through many lands. We travelled over tall mountains and through vast stretches of desert land. But all these details are not important. The important thing is that, at last, after a full year's journey we finally reached the court of the great Kublai Khan. He received us as royal visitors. By this time we had become most proficient in the Mongolian tongue and we were fortunately able to converse with him freely. Oh, there was so much he wanted to know! He asked hundreds of questions, for we were the very first people from Europe that he had ever seen. He asked us about the lands through which we had passed and he wanted to know about the kingdoms of Europe and how they were governed. He was curious about everything. He wanted to know about our religion. We answered all that he asked. He was interested in the Pope and he asked us to explain to him the Christian doctrine."

THE COURT OF KUBLAI KHAN

The Polo brothers explained to the Khan how the Christian religion differed from the religions in the Orient and they professed that Christianity was superior to all.

The Khan found the Polo brothers endowed with good sense and filled with worldly information. And so, after consulting with his ministers, the Khan decided to employ them as his ambassadors to the Pope.

Now Maffeo spoke: "Here are the letters which the Khan has written to the Pope. They ask the Pope to send to Cathay one hundred men of learning, thoroughly acquainted with the principles of Christianity, as well as the seven arts which form the bases of our culture. Several times we explained to the Khan that our seven arts include rhetoric, logic, grammar, arithmetic, astronomy, music and geometry. Now the Khan desires that these hundred learned men come to Cathay as his guests. While they are in Cathay he would like them to teach the scholars in his court all that they know. And in time, if these hundred men can prove that the religion of Christ is superior to all other religions, then the Khan promised that he, and all under him, would become Christians."

When these words were spoken the Polo brothers unpacked the costly gifts which Kublai Khan was sending to the Pope. These gifts they displayed to the astonished guests.

"And here," said Nicolo loosening the collar of his coat, "here is the golden tablet of authority given us by the Khan. This is inscribed in the Mongolian language and bears the seal of the emperor. Wherever we travelled in Cathay this golden talisman secured for us all that was necessary. We had but to command."

He held up the golden talisman for all to see. It was about as long as his hand though not as broad. This tag of pure beaten gold was suspended around his neck by a silken cord. Young Marco, who sat close to his father, could see the fine Mongolian engraving on this golden badge of authority. It was a strange script of a strange language.

Nicolo now opened the letters to the Pope which he had from the Khan and displayed the Khan's seal imprinted in royal vermilion.

After a brief silence one of the nobles at the table spoke: "You have been away, and at sea, and therefore you could not have heard the sad news. Only a few months ago our good Pope, Clement IV, died. The cardinals are now at this very moment journeying to Rome."

"This is indeed sad news," said Nicolo. "For now we will have to wait until a new Pope is elected. The Khan is determined to have one hundred learned men from Europe."

Later that night, when the guests had departed, young Marco asked to see again the Khan's golden tablet which enabled his envoys to demand all they required on their journey. This was truly a wonderful thing. He examined it closely. His eyes were round with wonder.

"How long, Father, does it take to elect a new pope in Rome?" asked Marco.

"Not long," replied his father.

"Then you will be returning to the Khan in Cathay?"

"Yes, we have promised faithfully that we shall return."

Young Marco looked up at his father. "When you sail again," he said boldly, "then I will sail with you. I am ready."

"How are you ready?" asked his father.

"All these years I have not been idle. My tutors have been preparing me for the life of a merchant. They have taught me Persian, and I know how a vessel must sail. I understand the ropes and the sails. I can read a chart, measure the winds—and I know how to steer by the stars at night and by compass in the day. And besides all this I already have a fair knowledge of arithmetic, geography and history."

"Good," said his father. He was pleased with Marco, his accomplishments, his youthful enthusiasm. He was also pleased with Marco's appearance. Before him stood a growing youth of medium height with broad shoulders. His well-set head was covered with thick, dark curly hair. His eyes were brown, large and sparkling. His lips were well formed, his chin strong and his nose well shaped. His brow was clear and altogether there was about him an intelligence which radiated from his face. Nicolo Polo looked at his son and smiled.

"You have grown, you are strong," he said. "Yes, this time you shall go with us to the court of Kublai Khan."

It had been a wonderful day. Such a wonderful day. But now Marco's joy knew no bounds.

That night when young Marco closed his eyes he dreamed of far-off lands and of strange races of men. He dreamed of oriental wonders, of marvels and splendours.

He awoke early the next morning. From his bed he could see the rim of the sun mount the eastern horizon across the bay. How far east was the sun? How far east was Cathay?

Soon, very soon, he would be journeying eastward to that magical land of Cathay. This was the place of his heart's desire.

CHAPTER II

NO SCHOLARS FOR CATHAY

While the Polo brothers and young Marco waited in Venice, there were difficulties in Rome. The college of cardinals could not agree upon a successor to the late Pope. It usually takes only a few days or weeks to reach a decision. But now, in the year 1269, many months had gone by and still the cardinals could not decide upon the one whom they considered worthy of holding this high office.

"We must be patient. We must wait," said Marco's father. "And while we wait let us use our time to good advantage. Let us prepare ourselves for the long journey."

Marco entered eagerly into all their plans. He was filled with the expectation of this oriental journey. And he asked his father and uncle to teach him the Mongolian language, for he realized that it would be a great advantage to him to be able to speak with the Tartars in their own tongue. The lessons were immediately begun and Marco learned quickly and easily.

The boy was also eager to learn all that he could about the lands of the Orient from which his father and uncle had just returned. Of these eastern countries very little was at that time known in Europe. Marco asked endless questions and the elder Polos told him all they knew.

They also explained to him how it was that they were the first to penetrate into the mysterious East.

"It is known that in ancient times," Nicolo explained to his son, "there was a trade route that ran from the Orient through the Holy Land and on to Rome. The merchants of old traded in spices and silks which came from the East. But soon after the decline of the empire of Rome this trade route was closed. And during the long centuries that followed, no attempt was made to establish contact with the East. The high Caucasus, the Ural Mountains and the deep Russian forests formed a natural barrier. But oddly enough, the Tartar conquests have once more opened the way. The Tartars have cut roads through the forests; they have bridged the wild rivers and pierced the rocky mountains. And it is because of these military roads that your uncle and I were able to reach Cathay."

"It is all so interesting but so confusing," said Marco. "Here at home we have good reason to believe that the Tartars are a fierce heathen race who show no mercy to their enemies. They plunder, they kill. Yet you report that they have treated you kindly and with great consideration. And you say that they have learning and that their princes are well mannered! Truly, it is all most confusing."

"They treated us with great consideration," said his father. "When we return to their dominions and pass through their conquered lands you will learn something of their remarkable history and their sudden rise to power. You will see a new world that is completely different from the world you know."

Then Nicolo asked his son: "Do you know why we in Europe call these people Tartars, when in reality they are Mongols from the land of Mongolia north of Cathay? It is because the word *tartaros* in Greek means hell. And when these armies first broke through the mountain barriers, with all their savage fierceness, they were said to resemble devils. Not having any other name for them, we in Europe called them 'men from hell', or Tartars. But now we know that they come from far-off Mongolia."

Young Marco was eager to see these "men from hell" and decide for himself. Were they really so fierce? And was it dangerous to travel among them? Or would the golden tablet of Kublai Khan fully protect them on this long journey? When could they start? What was the news from Rome? Would the deadlock between the cardinals never end?

A whole year went by and no pope was elected. And then another half year went by and still there was no new pope.

Now the Polo brothers grew impatient. They knew that the great Khan would not be pleased with this delay. They feared that the Khan might suppose that they had broken their promise to him and that they had no intention of returning to his land. And since the Polos were the only men from Europe that the Khan had ever encountered, he might, because of this failure, believe that all men from Europe break their promises easily.

No. It was not possible to wait much longer. So they decided to gather together what they needed for their journey and make preparations for leaving. But still they hesitated. To arrive before Kublai Khan without those hundred learned men which he so ardently desired would be to fail in their mission. But not to arrive at all was also bad. At length they decided to wait until two full years had expired since the death of Pope Clement.

When these two years had passed they dared not delay another day. And so saying good-bye to all, they boarded their ship, weighed anchor and hoisted the sails. The journey was now begun. The bobbing bow turned eastward.

Marco stood in the prow of the vessel. He was happy. He looked out across the blue sea. Occasionally he glanced back at the proud city of Venice with its hundred islands, its winding canals and its arched bridges. All this he knew so well. But the lands far to the east, these mysterious lands he did not know.

The bow pounded against the choppy water and with each pound a salty spray filled the air. The air was fresh. The sky was broad. And the blue of the sea stretched on and on as far as his eyes could see.

At last, after two years of waiting, they were on their journey. Marco was fifteen years old when his father and uncle returned from the East. Now he was seventeen. And he was tall and strong.

BEGINNING OF THE JOURNEY

A light breeze carried them on. They steered at night by the aid of the stars, while during the day they used the compass and their charts. Now and then they touched at some Mediterranean port to take on fresh water and food. And sometimes they docked to unload some of their cargo. In this leisurely manner they passed many of the scattered Greek islands and in time they arrived at the coast of Syria. This coast was close to the land of Jerusalem. And along this coast they found the harbour of the city of Acre. It was this city that was once captured by Richard I and his brave crusading knights.

As they sailed slowly into the harbour, Marco noticed that many of the vessels, recognizing the flags and pennants of Venice, were signalling to them. At length a rowboat came alongside their vessel and the men cried out: "Messages have arrived from Rome! A new pope has been chosen!"

The high lords of the city were at the wharf to greet them. There was much excitement. Letters for the Polo brothers had been sent by fast galley. They were signed by the new pope, Gregory X, who commanded these envoys to return immediately to Rome. For this journey the fast war galley that had brought the letters stood waiting.

While the Polos did not relish this return after they had made so good a start on their long journey, still they were eager to have the Pope comply with the wishes of the Khan and send the hundred learned men to the East. And so, after instructing their sailors to bring their vessel with its cargo to Constantinople, they boarded the fast war galley. It started out at once. It darted swiftly out of the harbour.

The galley was manned by a hundred slaves, who groaned and chanted while they worked the heavy oars. Soldiers stood over them with whips. And another hundred slaves reclined on the decks ready to relieve those who wearied at their labour. The sharp prow parted the water in front and a long trail of foam was left behind. When the winds were favourable and the sails hoisted, it seemed to Marco that they almost flew over the smooth surface of the water. And when the sun went down and night covered them, even then the slaves were at their places chanting their songs to the rhythmic strokes of the oars.

In this manner they raced across the sea. And before many days had passed they arrived at their destination.

In Rome, Gregory X received them without delay. He dictated several letters addressed to the Khan and also charged the Polos with the delivery of handsome presents made of gold and crystal. But instead of the hundred scholars which the Khan desired, the Pope ordered two friars to go along with them. "These brothers," he said, "are men of letters and of science, besides being profound theologians. They have my authority to ordain priests, to consecrate bishops and to grant absolution. These two can do everything that a hundred might accomplish." Then he wished them all well on their long journey and dismissed them from his audience hall.

Once more the Polos started eastward. Now accompanied by two timid friars, who had never before been out of Rome, they made their way back to the coast of Syria. Here the party of five bought good pack horses and started out toward the land of Armenia. Some nights they slept in the open and some nights they found lodging.

But they had not travelled many days when they heard bad news. The sultan of Babylonia had invaded Armenia with a great army and this army had begun on its work of destruction. The two friars were terrified at this news and, fearing for their lives, decided that they could not possibly go any further.

"But the journey has hardly begun," urged Nicolo.

"For us it has now ended," spoke one of the friars.

"The Khan waits for you. He is eager to learn about Christianity. And is it not your vow to spread the teachings of Christ?"

But many years in the shelter of a monastery had made the friars fear the great world outside, and they argued this way and that. "Let the infidels come to Rome," they finally said.

So they entrusted to the Polos the special letters that the Pope had given them to be delivered to the Khan. Then turning their horses around they started back toward the coast of Syria with all possible speed.

The three Polos continued on their journey. They travelled by day and rested at night. Soon they were deep into the land and far away from those shores of the Mediterranean that touched the countries of Europe. Now they were entering the little-known lands of the East.

The elder Polos had been through these eastern lands before. But to young Marco these lands were all new, and as he rode along his sharp eyes saw many things that were interesting to him. He saw strange birds and strange animals. He witnessed strange customs and he heard strange tales. And everything that was new and curious he noted.

In the pocket of his coat young Marco carried note paper. And he kept records of everything he saw, everything he learned. He wrote down the names of the countries and cities through which they passed. And he wrote down many other things which he heard on the way and which he did not want to forget.

During his long journey he filled many sheets with many notes. And it was from these notes that—years later—he was able to put together a full account of his travels. That travel record remains to this day the greatest journey ever recorded.

CHAPTER III

FOUNTAINS OF OIL

THE FIRST COUNTRIES through which the Polos passed were Armenia and Turkey. These lands were the most westernly provinces of the Khan's vast empire. As they rode along on horseback they passed through fair pasture land where shepherds tended their flocks. When they came to a village they stopped to refresh themselves and to speak with the people. Marco was particularly interested in watching the craftsmen at their work. He saw how the rug weavers washed and dyed their wools and how they wove their marvellous rugs. He watched the metalworkers making trays, vessels and jewelry of brass and silver. He saw the potters at their wheels and the woodworkers carving intricate designs for screens and furniture. All these things fascinated him. And his father and uncle, who had seen all this before, were forced to urge him on. The journey ahead was a long one and they could not tarry.

After many days of travelling they came into eastern Turkey and in the distance they discovered a snow-covered mountain that seemed to reach to the very sky. As they came closer they met a shepherd and Marco spoke to him.

"It is the Mountain of the Ark," the shepherd said. "High on its peak, Noah's ark came to rest after the flood."

"Then that must be Mount Ararat?"

"We call it simply the Mountain of the Ark," said the shepherd. "And from the high slopes of this mountain descended into this valley all living things to repopulate the world devastated by the flood."

A R M E N I A

The shepherd was friendly and he told them of many things. But he was also curious. He wanted to know who they were and where they were going.

"We are Venetians and we are going eastward," said Marco, "into the land of Persia. Then farther. But tell me, friend, what land lies to the north?"

"To the north is Georgia, the land of the flowing fountain. In this land," continued the shepherd, "there is a fountain from which flows, not water, but a dark oily liquid. The people do not use this oil for food, but as an unguent for the cure of skin distempers in men and cattle, as well as for other complaints; and it is also good for burning. People come from distant parts to procure it. So abundant is this fountain that many camels arrive daily and carry away great jugs filled with this curious liquid."

Marco's father and uncle smiled at the shepherd's story. They were certain that no such fountain existed. They argued with the shepherd. They said that it was well known that only water could bubble from the earth. But the shepherd insisted that his story was true. He had met people who had seen this fountain and had used its oil to light their lamps.

Unbelievable as this tale seemed to Marco, he nevertheless wrote it down exactly as he heard it.

The Polos now journeyed on and in time they came to the land of Persia. They found the entire countryside devastated by war. The Tartars had invaded Persia and the people had fought a long and hopeless battle against the invaders.

One evening while journeying through the land of Persia, the Polos reached a city called Saba. Here they spent the night. And here they visited the tombs of the three Magi, who in ancient times had journeyed to Bethlehem. They inquired about these kings of long ago, but the villagers were unable to tell them anything. They said, however, that the priests at the fire worshippers' castle, which they would be passing, would probably be able to tell them.

After several days' journey the Polos came to the castle of the fire worshippers where they stayed as guests. The priests of the castle said that the reason they worshipped fire was because of the three Magi.

Their elder stepped forward to explain: "In ancient times, three kings from this country went to worship a certain prophet who was newly born. These kings carried with them gifts: gold, frankincense and myrrh. They carried these in order to ascertain whether the newborn prophet were a god, an earthly king or a physician. Thus they reasoned: if the child takes the gold, then surely he is a king. If he takes the incense, then he is a god. And if he takes the myrrh, he is a physician.

"They presented their gifts and the child accepted all three. This confused the Magi but nevertheless they knelt down and worshipped him, and when they were about to depart the infant gave them a small sealed box. Now they travelled into the desert for several days and, curious to know what was contained in the box, they broke the seal. The box contained a stone. This they thought most strange. Could it be possible that the child meant to mock them? What is a stone anyway? And so they threw it away. They cast it into a nearby pit and instantly—a spark being made by the hard stone striking a rock—the entire pit burst into flames.

"In the bright light of the flames one of the kings said: 'It is all now clear to me. This stone was a symbol. It was intended that we should remain as firm as a stone in the faith that we received from him.'

"Then they took some of the fire from the burning pit and carried it home. They placed it in their temple and they tended it carefully to keep it ever burning. They worshipped this fire as a holy thing to the end of their days. And the long generations that followed these three ancient kings continued to worship this fire and to make all their sacrifices to it. This holy flame has through these long years been kept alight. And we to-day take great care that it should never be extinguished."

This was the tale which the Polos heard from the lips of one of the priests in the castle of the fire worshippers.

Marco of course knew the story of the three Magi and how they came to Bethlehem to worship the Christ child, but he had never before heard of the stone which Christ had given the kings, nor of the holy fire.

After resting for two days at the castle of the fire worshippers, the Polos again started on their journey. They now travelled for many days through fertile lands where they saw great fields of cotton, wheat, barley, millet and other grains. They saw rich vineyards and fine orchards.

It was in this district that Marco saw the strangest sheep in all the world. He noted that they were very large—almost twice as large as ordinary sheep—with long, thick tails. These tails, which weighed up to thirty pounds, were meaty and excellent to eat. These sheep are known to-day as fat-tailed sheep.

Here, too, Marco saw many colourful birds—swift falcons with reddish breasts, turtledoves, pheasants, and black-and-white-peppered partridges with red beaks and legs. He pointed them out to his father and uncle. He had a great interest in birds and animals.

Then leaving this fertile land the travellers reached a small salt desert on the eastern border of Persia. It took them eight long days and nights to cross this arid wasteland. They were required to carry sufficient food for themselves and grain for their beasts, for in this desert there were no towns, no inns and no water. And when on the eighth day they saw fertile fields ahead, they knew that all danger was past and they were happy.

Chapter IV

HASHISH—AND "ASSASSINS"

Leaving Persia and entering Afghanistan, the Polos came to a mountainous country where the people told a tale of a strange tyrant. For many years the countryside had been terrorized by this despot. Only twenty years before had he been overthrown and killed. And there were many who remembered him and now dared to speak freely of his violence.

Marco Polo recorded the story as he and his father and uncle heard it from the people of this land. It concerned a man who was called Sheik al-Jabal, which translated means Old Man of the Mountain.

Many years ago a sheik of Arabia, who was the supreme ruler of his tribe, was forced to flee from his enemies in Egypt. His whole tribe followed him. And when they came to this wild mountainous country in Afghanistan they happened into a beautiful narrow valley where, high above on a rocky cliff, they saw the castle fortress of Alamut. They stormed this castle and took it by force.

The sheik now caused stone walls and fortifications to be built on both ends of the ravine to make this fortress secure against all enemies. In the beautiful valley he created luxurious gardens with fruit trees, fragrant shrubs, flowers and fountains. In these gardens he built fresh-water pools and a number of little palaces which he furnished with treasures of gold and silver, with furniture, paintings, silk hangings and rare rugs. All these things he and his tribe had looted from passing caravans.

When these pleasure gardens and palaces were finished and provided with all the luxuries which he could devise, the sheik selected the most beautiful young girls of the tribe to live here. He chose those who were accomplished in the arts of singing, dancing and the playing of musical instruments. He provided these girls with rich dresses and ornaments. They were cared for and guarded by matrons who lived indoors and were seldom seen in the gardens.

The sheik was a cruel master and ruled with an iron hand. He instructed his priests to teach all the young children of his tribe that he was the chief prophet of Mohammed and must be worshipped, for he alone had the power of allowing those who died to enter paradise. The children believed their priests and grew up to hold their sheik in holy reverence.

Now to defend his mountain castle and keep a constant watch for enemy invaders, the sheik took into the castle a troop of young men. He selected only those who were strong, obedient and displayed courage. These young men performed daily exercises and were trained by their captains to serve as castle guards. At the same time, the priests gave them religious instruction and repeated over and over that the sheik was their supreme ruler, that he was the prophet of Mohammed and that he alone could secure their admission to paradise. Therefore, in all matters must they please their sheik, otherwise they would find the gates of paradise closed.

The priests of this tribe were not only masters of religious matters but also had a knowledge of drugs. From the leaves of hemp they made a drug called hashish.

At times the Old Man of the Mountain would order that this drug be placed in the food of a dozen or more young men who were being trained as castle guards. Then when these youths were completely drugged—and unconscious—they were carried down into the valley and brought into the secret garden palaces.

In a few hours, when the effects of the drug began to wear off, the young men opened their eyes and found themselves surrounded by luxuries greater than anything they could ever imagine. Each youth,

HE OLD MAN OF THE MOUNTAIN

on recovering from the stupor caused by the drug, found himself attended by several lovely damsels, who played soothing music, sang and danced. As soon as he was fully awake they fed him dishes of great delicacy which they served with fine wines. And they coaxed him to indulge in all the pleasures he desired. So fully were these youths intoxicated with pleasures that they truly believed that they had been transported to paradise.

These extreme pleasures continued for about five days; then once more the youths were secretly drugged and carried back up the mountain to the fortress. When they awoke, the sheik came to their couch and asked them where they had been.

"Through your kind favour, your Highness, we have been allowed to visit paradise." This was the reply all gave.

Then the priests who were always present at these occasions said: "We have the assurance of our holy prophets that he who defends him and obeys his wishes shall inherit paradise. Only if you are devoted and obedient to his orders will happiness a paradise again come to you."

At this, one and all replied that they were ready to receive the commands of their master. He had but to order them—and even if they were to die, they would die happily in the service of the holy sheik.

Now the Old Man of the Mountain made lists of his enemies, including those neighbouring princes which he did not like. And he sent out these youths whom he had so strictly disciplined. They carried with them concealed daggers and vowed never to return until the deed was accomplished. These fanatical young men brought terror to all the surrounding countries. Because of the drug, hashish, which they ate, these terrorists were named Hashishins. But this name was difficult to pronounce and soon the people in the terrorized lands called them Assassins. The first "assassins" in the world were those trained youths of the Old Man of the Mountain who ruled over the castle fortress.

Now it happened that when the Tartar governor of this province heard about the Old Man of the Mountain and his trained assassins, he sent an army into these lands. The army at once set siege to the castle stronghold. But since the castle on its rocky perch was almost inaccessible and could be easily defended, the commanding Tartar officer kept the castle surrounded in order to save unnecessary loss of his men. Thus he starved the Hashishins into submission. It was a slow way, but a sure one. After several years, when all the provisions in the fortress were exhausted, the besieged opened the gates and surrendered. The Old Man of the Mountain and his followers were put to death by the Tartar soldiers, his mountain fortress was demolished and his garden of paradise destroyed.

During the long siege quite a number of this drug-eating tribe managed to escape from the rocky ravine. Some were reported seen in Syria, and some were said to have crossed over the high mountains and taken refuge in northern India.

All this strange history the Polos learned from the people with whom they spoke. For years these people had lived in terror. Now they were free. The iron rule of the Old Man of the Mountains was finally destroyed.

CHAPTER V

BONES GUIDE THE TRAVELLER

LEAVING THE LAND of the Old Man of the Mountain the travellers passed through a well-inhabited country, very beautiful and abounding in fruit, corn and vines. But the people were treacherous and the Polos were in constant danger of their lives.

After several more weeks of travelling they reached the province which was called Balashan. When they entered this province they were entering the western edge of a territory which lies north of India and runs eastward to the border of China. This territory remains to this day one of the most primitive outposts of civilization. And very few travellers since the Polos have ever attempted to explore this land. Marco Polo was the very first European traveller to cross this territory and leave a record of his experiences.

The province of Balashan is a rugged country where there are many mountains with lofty peaks, rapid rivers and deep ravines. Here the Polos found many wild beasts and strange animals. And the people, too, were strange and wild.

This land was ruled by a prince who claimed to be a descendant of Alexander the Great, through his marriage with the daughter of Darius, King of the Persians. It was claimed that here was a strain of horses stemming directly from Alexander's famous horse Bucephalus. All the colts were foaled with a particular mark on the forehead.

Marco Polo was told that in the mountains about were found precious rubies and the beautiful blue stone called lapis lazuli. The rubies,

THE PRECIOUS STONES OF BALASHAN

imbedded in the high mountains, were mined in the same manner as gold and silver. The lapis lazuli was found running in broad veins. Here, too, were mines of silver, copper and lead.

Marco Polo recorded that the people of this country were good archers and clothed themselves with the skins of wild animals. He was impressed by the many falcons and other species of birds which he saw in the sky and by the great numbers of wild sheep which rambled in flocks of four, five and six hundred.

Leaving this province of Balashan, Marco, with his father and uncle, came to a great barrier of mountains.

For days on end they climbed one range after another, ascending higher and higher, until at last they reached a point in the road where Marco felt that the surrounding peaks must be the highest lands in all the world. And it was here, between two ranges, that they came upon a large lake from which a river flowed into a great plain covered with rich grass.

For twelve days the Polos travelled across this lofty plain, which is called the Pamir Plateau. And during all these days they did not see any habitations. They did, however, come upon isolated herdsmen tending their cattle.

One night the Polos sat around a campfire and talked with a herdsman. Marco, having seen many large wild mountain sheep, with great twisted horns, in this district was curious to know about them.

"Why are there so many skeletons and horns of these beautiful sheep lying about the countryside?" asked Marco. "You herdsmen do not kill them, do you?"

"Oh, no," said the herdsman. "Only occasionally do we kill a sheep for food. But this country is filled with marauding wolves and these wolves kill large numbers of them."

"It is a great pity," said Marco.

"No, it does not really matter," spoke the herdsman. "For there are so many of these sheep. And besides, their bones and horns are useful to us. We make ladles and bowls from their horns. And as you have undoubtedly noticed, as you travelled along, we also use these horns for building corrals for our cattle."

The herdsman then reached into a great leather sack and drew out some bowls and ladles to show the Polos. Marco felt that these utensils were rather crude, but he thought that the herdsmen were very clever to utilize the old horns in this manner.

The herdsman spoke again. "We herdsmen also gather up the scattered bones and horns of these dead sheep and make heaps of them at the side of the road. You must have seen them. We do this as a guide for travellers in the winter when the way is covered with snow."

Sitting beside the campfire that night Marco made careful notes of everything the herdsman had said and of everything he had seen. Among the things he recorded was the fact that campfires at this high altitude did not seem to give off as much heat as fires in lower country. He also wrote a description of the mountain sheep, with great twisted horns, that lived in this country. But he did not know as he sat there writing that he was the first traveller to make a record of this animal.

When these sheep were again discovered by modern explorers, they found them to be exactly as Marco Polo had described them. And in his honour then named them *Ovis Poli* which means simply Marco Polo's sheep.

The following morning as the Polos travelled on along this high tableland, they could see several of the snow covered peaks of the proud Himalayas. Some of these lofty peaks—the highest in the world—rise over twenty five thousand feet. And Marco noted that no birds could be seen near their summits.

At the end of twelve days, the travellers came to the end of the green plateau and for forty days more they travelled on toward Cathay over mountains and through valleys, crossing over range after range. In all these forty days they did not see a house or even a hut or any other sign of human life. Fortunately, they had been warned of this extreme desolation and so carried with them provisions which they divided into daily rations.

O V I S P O L

These rations proved just sufficient to see them through. And they considered themselves most fortunate in not encountering a delaying snowstorm. For here and there as they travelled, they passed the bones of travellers who had perished on the way.

At length the Polos reached the eastern end of that strange territory that begins at Balashan and which lies just north of India. They reached the city of Kashgar.

Now they were on the soil of Cathay and under the direct rule of Kublai Khan. Now they could draw out that precious golden talisman and in the name of the great emperor demand provisions, lodgings, horses—all they desired for their long journey.

At last Marco was in the land of the great Khan. Cathay was old. Cathay was great. Cathay was strange and wonderful.

CHAPTER VI

"SALAMANDER" CLOTH

KASHGAR WAS THE most westerly city of Cathay. And after the Polos had rested here for several days, they started out again on their journey eastward. They found the country through which they passed well populated and rich with farm lands. Here the inhabitants cultivated gardens and vineyards, as well as cotton, flax, hemp and grain. They also passed many mountain streams in which they found precious jade. This jade was found here in many varieties and in great quantities.

Marco noted three interesting things about the people of this countryside, the most important of which was their religious freedom. To one who came from Medieval Europe this religious tolerance was an unknown thing. Here he found three forms of worship. Some worshipped Mohammed, some worshipped Buddha and some, to Marco's surprise, worshipped Christ. These religions, he found, existed side by side in peace. This freedom of worship, traditional in Cathay, was supported by the great Khan. The Khan allowed religions to be freely practised.

But who were these Christians that Marco found here in far Cathay? Marco inquired about them and found that they were called Nestorian Christians. They were the followers of a certain abbot, Nestorius, who at a very early date—about four hundred years after the death of Christ—broke with the Church of Rome. His beliefs and teachings varied slightly from the dogma of Rome. For this he was persecuted and driven from his church. But he had many loyal followers and wherever they went they brought his teachings and built their churches. After the fifth century, some of them came into Cathay where they found complete religious freedom. They remained here and by the time Marco Polo arrived their church was well established on oriental soil.

The second thing of interest which Marco noted here in western Cathay was that many of the people had large swellings on their necks. And he recorded that these were "occasioned by the quality of the water." To-day medical science has confirmed the fact that pure mountain water, far from the sea and therefore lacking in iodine, is the cause of this swelling which is called goiter. This illness is prevalent, even to-day, in western China.

The third thing which Marco noted was a strange regulation. In a province called Pein there was a twenty-day law. If a man travelled away from his home and was absent for twenty days or more, then his wife had the right, if she were so inclined, to take another husband. This new husband at once became the master of her home!

At the end of twenty-eight days of travelling through fertile country, the Polos came to the city of Lop, at the edge of an arid section which was called the Desert of Lop. Here camels were used for beasts of burden, for they were able to ride the desert far better than horses or asses.

After transferring their packs to camels and securing—by means of the golden tablet—provisions for a full thirty days' journey, Marco Polo and his father and uncle joined a caravan. The caravan masters promised to protect them across the desert. They knew the desert well and they promised to manage the journey so that the caravan would be brought to rest each evening beside an oasis of fresh water.

But before starting out on this desert, and while still in the city of Lop, the Polos heard many strange stories of fears, terrors and spirits.

"There are evil spirits in the desert," warned some of the people of Lop. "These spirits lure travellers from their route and bring them to destruction."

THE DESERT OF LO

"Do not stray from your caravan," cautioned others, "for it is then that the spirits do their evil work. They will call out your names as though they were your friends calling to you, and following these voices you will be led in the wrong direction and hopelessly lost."

Still others told how sometimes at night a lonely traveller would hear the sound of the march of a large caravan. At daybreak he would pursue in this direction, hoping to join the caravan. Thus he would be led far into the desert where he would wander and perish.

The Polos did not fully believe these tales of evil spirits. But when their caravan was out in the desert they did hear strange noises at night. These sounds, Marco recorded, resembled a variety of musical instruments all playing at once. Now and then, added to the sounds of these instruments was the booming of drums. And such noises, breaking into the silence of the desert night, were indeed frightening.

To-day we know that the sounds which the Polos heard—and which so frightened the people of Lop—are caused by the hot sands cooling quickly at sundown. The contraction and settling of large areas of sand will at times produce strange noises which resemble the sound of musical instruments.

Very few travellers, to this day, have crossed the desolate, bone-strewn desert waste of Lop. And Marco, together with his father and uncle, were happy when this crossing was over and they came once more into friendly villages.

It was here, also, in the western part of Cathay that Marco noted a custom that seemed to him very strange. In the first place, these people did not bury their dead, but cremated them. Furthermore, when someone died his relations did not immediately hold funeral services. These people first called together their temple priests and their local astrologers. The astrologers drew a horoscope, which showed the position of the heavenly planets and stars at the time of the birth of the person who was now dead. From this chart they calculated the lucky days and months and decided on one day which they believed to be the most fortunate for the deceased to make his entrance in to heaven. Accordingly, they might order that the funeral be delayed for weeks or even, in some cases, for as long as six months.

In order to preserve a body for so long a time, it was the custom to build a coffin of stout planks several inches thick. The joints were sealed with a mixture of tar and lime. With the body was placed a quantity of sweet-scented gums, camphor and other drugs. After all was tightly sealed, the raw coffin boards were covered with coloured silk. Then a small table was placed before the coffin. On this table were bread, wine and dishes of food. This food was for the spirit of the dead person who must wait for his lucky day before he could leave this earth and enter heaven.

At last, when the long awaited day arrived, the relatives and friends formed a funeral procession and the coffin was carried out into the country to the place of cremation. On the way, the procession rested under silken canopies which had been set up along the road. Here, at these resting places, the relatives and friends burned a quantity of cardboard money, paper figures of men and women, horses and all those other things which they wanted the dead person to have. The spirits of these paper images they believed would rise to heaven and bring comfort to the departed soul. Thus he would have money when he got to heaven and he would also have horses, servants and friends.

At first Marco thought that this strange burial custom was but a local rite. But later on he discovered that it was common to all Cathay. This custom dates back to ancient times—and what Marco Polo saw is still practised in Cathay to this very day.

Here, too, in western Cathay, Marco witnessed the weaving of a fabric which he called salamander cloth. This was a kind of cloth woven from mineral fibres which resembled a coarse wool. A fossil substance was mined in the mountains and Marco Polo describes the process as follows: "This, after being exposed to the sun to dry is pounded in a brass mortar, and is then washed until all the earthly particles are separated. The fibre thus cleansed and detached from each other, they then spin into thread and weave into cloth." To bleach this cloth it was then thrown into an open flame and it came out white as snow.

It was believed, in Marco Polo's time, that the salamander was a lizard that could resist fire, and because of this Marco called this cloth salamander cloth. But to-day we know this mineral wool by the name of asbestos.

Of the strange animals which Marco Polo found in this part of the world, one was the musk deer and the other was the yak. Marco noted that the musk deer was small, the size of a gazelle, with coarse hair. He was the first to describe this strange little deer which gives its life for a breath of perfume. He recorded that it had no horns but had two tusks on its upper jaw. The musk was contained in a little sac, under the hide, on the belly of the animal. When the animal was killed this valuable little sac was cut out and dried in the sun. It had a most pungent odour and was used in Cathay as a base for perfume. And to-day, centuries later, the best French perfumes all contain a little of this musk which comes from this special deer in Tibet and western China.

The yak, Marco said, was large, sometimes six feet high. It looked very much like an ugly bull, but its legs were shorter and had long, soft hair. But like a bull the yak could be very ugly and dangerous. Marco saw many that were wild and quite a few that had been tamed and made into beasts of burden. These animals were very strong; they could carry great loads on their backs and pull the cart as easily as a large workhorse.

Besides these two strange animals, Marco found in this part of Cathay a pure white camel. The hair of this camel was woven into fine cloth by the natives and sold to merchants who sent it to many parts of the Orient. This luxurious cloth was highly prized.

Here, too, Marco saw great flocks of a special kind of pheasant. This bird was most beautiful and its tail feathers were often six feet long. On the stage the heroes of Chinese drama often, to this day, wear these enormous plumes in their hats.

All these things Marco saw and recorded. They were new to him, they were strange, they were different.

And each day as the Polos drew closer to the great eastern cities of Cathay and the court of the emperor Kublai Khan, Marco noticed that the roads grew much better. He was later to learn that the Khan felt that the prosperity and safety of his land depended largely upon an extensive and well-regulated highway system.

Over good roads merchants could transport their wares to all parts of the land. And over these same roads troops could be quickly moved from one section to another in times of danger. He also felt that a system of highways helped to unite the people of his country.

He therefore caused to be built a network of roads throughout Cathay. These roads, patrolled by soldiers for the protection of travellers, connected all the provinces and cities of the land. Large gangs of labourers were constantly employed to keep these highways in repair. And for the comfort of travellers, the Khan had trees planted along all the main thoroughfares. These trees gave shade in the summer and held back the snow in winter. In the arid lands, where the trees would not grow, the Khan ordered stone columns to be erected to mark the way when snow covered the countryside.

Marco recorded that he and his father and uncle found many inns along the road that were most comfortable. They also stayed at government posthouses, where they secured—with the aid of their golden talisman—fresh horses and all else that they required.

These posthouses were run by the government for the benefit and comfort of all travellers, those who travelled on their own business as well as those who travelled for the government. Each posthouse contained sleeping quarters and all necessary provisions for the travellers. Those who travelled on the Khan's business were accommodated without cost.

Stables were attached to each posthouse and here fresh horses could be exchanged for weary ones. Some of these stables contained as many as four thousand horses so that fast postriders of the Khan could proceed without delay. Ambassadors, governors and other officials of the land could by this means cover great distances in the shortest possible time.

The Polos travelled on.

Besides the Persian and Mongolian languages which Marco Polo already knew, and in which he had become proficient, now, in this land of western Cathay which is directly north of India, he heard two more languages. These were Chinese and the language of the Hindus called Hindustani.

Marco at once set to work to learn these oriental tongues.

At every chance he spoke with the natives, and from them he also learned to write the peculiar scripts. He filled many pages with exercises which he could practice.

In Cathay there were very few who were acquainted with the four main languages of the orient. Each of these four languages—Persian, Mongolian, Chinese and Hindustani—were spoken by great multitudes in the East. And the Khan was the supreme emperor over their vast territories. Communication was important for his rule. And language, he knew, was the key to communication.

All this, as we will soon discover, was to make Marco Polo very important in the eyes of Kublai, the great Khan.

CHAPTER VII

THE STORY OF GENGHIS KHAN

HE POLOS TRAVELLED on and on, day after day, eastward toward the court of Kublai Khan. One day they came to the Great Wall of China. This was a sight unlike any Marco had ever seen.

The travellers paused on the crest of a hill. Before them stretched, as far as they could see, a gigantic serpent of masonry. It stretched eastward and westward, from edge to edge of the horizon, winding its way over mountains and through valleys and across broad plains.

When the Polos came to one of the gates in the Great Wall they stopped to rest and Marco spoke with the gatekeeper.

"How long is this wall?" he asked.

"It is long," said the gatekeeper. "Very long. It stretches all the way from the sea to the far west, a distance of about eighteen hundred miles. And it was built many years ago, centuries ago.

"How many centuries?" Asked Marco.

"Almost too many to count. It is about fifteen hundred years old."

This was old indeed, thought Marco. Even before the days of Christ this wall was begun. About two hundred years before.

Marco appraised the wall. He examined the blocks of masonry and then he and the gatekeeper climbed a stairway to the top. He estimated that the wall was about twenty-two feet high and about twenty feet wide. From the top of the wall he could see look-out towers which were spaced one hundred yards apart. These towers were forty feet tall. And the gatekeeper told him that here and there, along the great stretch of wall, were arched gateways secured by heavy oaken doors.

THE TARTARS

Then Marco asked why this wall had been built and by whom.

"Ah!" said the gatekeeper. "It was built by the people of Cathay and for a very good reason. It was built to keep out the savage Mongolians from the North. These warlike tribes from Mongolia were constantly harrying the peaceful lands of Cathay. And so the wall was built to keep out the enemy. And it succeeded in doing so for many centuries, as long as the Mongolian tribes were not united. But one day a leader, Genghis Khan—the grandfather of the present Khan-Kublai—united the scattered tribes and, with these Mongolian hordes, stormed through the gates in the wall and conquered Cathay."

Marco was curious to know more and the gatekeeper continued.

"Ah, it was simple indeed. It was done at night. A miserable gatekeeper was bribed and the gates were opened to the enemy. A single act of treachery and the labour and sweat of centuries was made worthless."

All this was most interesting, for Marco realised that this was the very same Genghis Khan and his Mongolian hordes which swept across Asia and brought terror to Europe. These were the same people who in Europe called Tartars.

He asked the gatekeeper to tell him more.

Then as they stood there looking at the great Wall of China, the gatekeeper told Marco everything he knew about Genghis Khan, the greatest conqueror since Alexander. And to the gatekeepers account Marco added many things that he knew about the Tartars in Europe.

"It is a cruel history written in blood," said the gatekeeper. "It is the story of the great rise of a simple shepherd boy from the plains of Mongolia." Then he told Marco the story of Genghis.

Born the son of a petty chieftain on the Plains of Mongolia, Genghis spent his childhood in the saddle rounding up cattle and horses. His people were nomads. They moved along with their cattle. Where the grass was green, there they stayed. Their home was a tent.

But the tents of the Mongols were different. In the first place, each was mounted on a wooden platform which had wheels like a cart, so that it would be drawn by oxen or tamed yaks. The tents were made of thick felt supported by strips of wood woven in basket fashion. On top of each was an opening to allow for ventilation. The felt was treated with butter fat which made it waterproof, and heavy cords held the tent firm against the wind.

Some of the tents, mounted on broad moving platforms, were so large that they required many beasts to pull them along. Whole families lived in a single tent.

In the summer the people dressed in woollen cloth which was home spun and loomed. In the winter they wore the fur of animals. The men and women were hardened. They were wonderful hunters and expert horsemen. They rode long-stirrup, in almost a standing position. And they were able to remain in the saddle a whole day without fatigue. No horsemen in the entire world could equal them.

Now it happened that when Genghis was only thirteen years old his father died suddenly. At once the chiefs of neighbouring tribes desired to make themselves masters over this tribe who had lost its chieftain.

"We will protect you," said some.

"Come, join us and we will all be one family," others pleaded.

But the widowed mother answered them: "My son Genghis will rule. He will be chief of the tribe."

"He is young. Your people need a leader. They will rise up against you."

"In his father's place, Genghis will rule," repeated his mother.

"The deepest wells are sometimes dry, and the hardest stone is sometimes broken. Why should your people cling to you when they are without a leader? And then, too, there are those who might attack you."

But the child Genghis did not wait for enemies to attack him. He set out at once to train and arm the young men of his tribe. Then selecting the weakest of his neighbouring tribes he swooped down upon it without warning. His attack was sudden, swift and merciless. He was victorious.

In this manner he conquered one tribe after another until he had consolidated many Mongolian tribes.

He persuaded those whom he conquered to fight with his men and conquer others. Soon all Mongolia was under his rule, all except one section ruled over by an old chieftain. Genghis went to him and asked for the hand of his daughter in marriage.

"After all, are we not all Mongols?" he said. "Why must we fight among ourselves? We should be one, for then we would be strong and able to resist any enemy."

As soon as he married the daughter of this chieftain Genghis was recognized as ruler of all Mongolia. Now he cast his eyes across the Great Wall of China. Cathay was rich. His men were now battle trained; they were veterans of many campaigns; they had developed special military manoeuvres and new strategies. They were swift. They were fierce. They were merciless. He decided he was ready to invade great Cathay.

Secretly, Genghis Khan massed his men along a secluded part of the Great Wall. After bribing one of the gatekeepers he rode his whole army, all mounted on good horses, through a gate at night. In the morning began a war of terror. Village after village was set afire and those who did not flee were struck down and killed.

Genghis believed in lightning-swift strokes. He believed in surprise attacks. He believed in conquering his enemy by sheer force and terror.

The emperor of China and his court fled from old Peking and sought refuge in southern Cathay. The people of Cathay were unprepared to fight this ruthless enemy. And so it was not long before Genghis, who was still a young man, declared himself ruler of Cathay as well as Mongolia.

Now elated by success and drunk with victory, Genghis moved his armies westward. Never before had so fierce an army crossed so wide a land. Never before had an army been so well trained and organized. Often, in forced marches, the advance soldiers would each have eight horses. The rider would change mounts every hour. Thus they were able to ride day and night without resting. Sometimes these warriors dozed in their saddles, but they rode on and on. And when hungry they would pause for a brief moment, open a vein in their horse's leg and, after drinking some blood, they would bind up the horse's wound and ride on.

Genghis divided his forces into three armies. As generals to lead his right army Genghis appointed his brothers. His sons commanded the left army, while he himself, with the aid of his youngest son, headed the central army. These three armies, although completely independent of each other, were united by his single supreme command. They joined forces whenever necessary.

Genghis developed new military manoeuvres and strategies. He believed in long and thorough preparations, surprise attacks and the power of terror. He sometimes used his central army for attack. Then when the enemy would come to grips with this force, his two side armies would suddenly appear and, like a nutcracker, squeeze the life out of the foe.

Another war manoeuvre developed by Genghis was that of sending a small force ahead while his main forces remained behind. This small force, purposely encountering the enemy, would feign that they were hopelessly outnumbered and retreat. The enemy, certain that they could overwhelm so smaller force, would pursue them and thus be drawn into a well-designed trap. They soon found themselves completely surrounded and hopelessly outnumbered.

With these tactics the Mongolian armies of Genghis marched victoriously from one end of Asia to the other. Their barbarous cruelty struck terror in the hearts of all. And all the lands they conquered became part of the empire of Genghis Khan.

At length, when most of Asia was his and his armies came to the borders of Greater Turkey, Genghis decided that he now had enough territory. He sent a message of peace to the shah of Turkey.

"I have no need of other lands," he wrote in this message. "I take it that we have an equal interest in encouraging trade between our subjects."

The shah seemed agreeable. But the first trading party, sent across the border by Genghis, was seized by the governor of one of the Turkish cities and the members of this party were put to death as spies.

Genghis at once demanded satisfaction. He demanded the head of the governor. But now the shah grew arrogant, and not only did he refuse to surrender the governor but he cut off the heads of the Tartar envoys, whom Genghis had sent with his demand. These heads he returned to Genghis with his best compliments.

In this way wars often begin. Diplomacy fails because pride prevents mistakes from being acknowledged. Tactlessness leads to arrogance. Arrogance to insult. An insult leads to war.

Genghis vowed that he would have his revenge. This revenge was destined to set into motion a military campaign which was one of the most startling in the history of the world. This campaign not only changed the map of part of the world but brought the Mongolians and the Turks into Europe. All Western civilization trembled.

Genghis did not begin his campaign against the shah without careful preparations. He felt the heat of the insult; but he acted with cool deliberation. He waited until the spring of the year before he sent one of his armies into Turkey. Against this army the shah led a force of four hundred thousand men, but in the battles that followed they were completely routed, with more than a third of their number slain. As the shah retreated with what could be saved of his army, he was suddenly confronted by a fresh Mongolian force that appeared without warning before him. This he had not counted on. And still a third Mongolian army invaded Turkey to set fire to the cities and villages and slay all—men, women and children.

Now the shah fled in terror. No place was safe. And nowhere could he remain very long. At one time he was forced to disguise himself as a poor wandering priest and seek refuge from mosque to mosque.

One after another the proud and rich walled cities of his land were besieged. Sometimes a siege lasted five or six months before the city, through sheer hunger, would be forced to surrender. Such a long siege befell the city of Bokhara. When finally the Mongols entered, Genghis was at the head of his troops. He drove his horse up the steps of the central mosque and from the terrace called out to his men: "The hay is cut; give your horses fodder." This was his way of saying that the work was done and now his soldiers were free to kill and plunder. From their proud city not a single person escaped alive. The city was stripped of everything of value, then burnt to the ground. But still the shah was pursued. At length, reduced to a beggar, and almost alone, the shah in his flight reached the shore of the Caspian Sea. Here, due to long exposure and grief, he died.

But the news of the shah's death did not reach Genghis whose armies continued in pursuit, devastating everything in their path. Whole multitudes of Turkish people, in fear of the advancing enemy, fled westward into Europe. Such is the power of insult.

The Mongolian armies now crossed the Caucasian Mountains into Russia. They cut broad roads through the forests over which they drove their tented carts. Now they came to the vast Russian plains which offered rich grazing lands for their horses and cattle.

The proud Russian cities of Kiev and Moscow were besieged for many months and when they fell all were slain—all except the young girls who were taken captive and sold as slaves.

But still insult burnt in the heart of Genghis and he marched his armies on. The king of Poland trembled. In his desperation he called for aid against these barbarous invaders. He wrote to the Pope that the name of Christianity was threatened with complete extinction. But no aid was sent. Poland fell and the king fled.

Now the cities of Hungary were brought to ruin. And with the coming of winter the armies of Genghis set up their camps on the eastern bank of the Danube River. Here they waited for spring.

Europe was weak. The Dark Ages were still over the people. Centuries of ignorance had enfeebled them. Centuries of superstitions and strange religious doctrines had destroyed their sense of reality and their will to resist invaders. The Moors had already come into Spain and encountered little resistance. What was to prevent the Tartars in their victorious westward march?

But strange as it may seem, when spring arrived the Tartars did not advance across the Danube. In fact they began to draw their armies back into Asia. This was a great relief to Europe. But the reason for this retreat the Europeans did not know.

However, there was a good reason. And this reason Marco Polo now learned—among the many other things that he learned about this amazing conqueror Genghis. The Mongolian armies did not continue their advance upon Europe, for that winter, after a brief illness, the great Genghis suddenly died.

His death was kept secret. His body was moved in a great funeral procession all the way across Asia to his homeland in Mongolia. To prevent the news of his death from being known, all people on the road who happened to see the passing funeral procession were captured and killed. It is recorded that in this march twenty thousand innocents were slain.

Genghis was buried in a secret grave with all the primitive religious rites of the Mongolians. And even to this day the exact location of his burial place remains unknown.

Born the son of a simple nomad chieftain, Genghis had lived to build the greatest military machine that the world had known. He lived to see his victorious armies spread over the entire breadth of Asia and over a good part of Europe. He had made himself ruler over more territory than any emperor in the entire history of the world. He established principles of war which were new and ruthless. He made war on whole populations, as well as upon the armed enemy.

When Genghis died, in the year 1227, his grandson Kublai was only thirteen years old. But he had already been on campaigns with his conquering grandfather. And at a very early age he learned the art of Mongolian warfare.

Now, forty-seven years after his grandfather's death, Kublai was on the throne of this vast empire. And he was waiting eagerly for the return of those Italian merchants whom he had sent to the Pope as his envoys. He was waiting patiently for those hundred men of learning whom he hoped might come to his court. He knew that it was a long journey from Cathay to Rome and back. Still so many years had passed since the Polo merchants had left that the Khan had now almost given up hope of ever seeing them again.

But one day his couriers brought word that the Polo merchants, together with a young son of one of the brothers, were reported on the road that led to his court. However, they were still some distance away, a distance that would require a journey of forty more days.

At this news the Khan was happy. He sent out officers on fresh horses to greet the weary travellers and to see that they had everything they required for their comfort. And he ordered these officers to escort the Polos to his palace with the least possible delay.

This they did. Under royal escort the Polos now rode forward to the capital of Cathay.

On the ruins of old Peking, once laid waste by the terrible Genghis, Kublai Khan, his grandson, had built a new city. This city, the capital of his vast empire, was named Cambalu, which in Mongolian means “City of the Khan”.

Here, in a magnificent marble palace, surrounded by great luxuries and vast treasures gathered from distant lands, Kublai Khan waited patiently for the arrival of the Polos.

CHAPTER VIII

"WHERE ARE THE HUNDRED MEN OF LEARNING?"

In the great audience hall of the palace, the three Polos knelt before the Khan. They bowed their heads to the carpet four times. But the Khan quickly ordered them to rise and made them welcome.

He was pleased to have his envoys back at court. They had kept their word and returned to him, in spite of so long a journey beset with great dangers and many hardships.

As soon as the Khan had finished with his words of welcome, Nicolo presented his son.

"May it please your Majesty; this is my son Marco. He is here to serve you."

Marco bowed respectfully.

The Khan smiled. There was something about Marco's bright face which he liked. And the Khan was quick to recognize the intelligent sparkle in his eyes.

He asked Marco many questions and was pleased to hear how fluently he spoke Mongolian. And when Kublai learned that the young Marco also spoke Persian, Hindustani and Chinese he was greatly impressed. He said that in a day or two, when the travellers were fully rested, he wanted to see them again. He wanted especially to speak to Marco and hear of all the adventures they had had on their long journey cast. The Khan said that he was curious to know about the many people in his vast kingdom. These people belonged to him. He was their ruler. And he was eager to know everything about them.

KUBLAI KHAN

While the Khan spoke Marco noted that he was quite heavy. Still he was of middle stature; that is, he was neither too tall nor too short. His body was in good proportion and his complexion fair. His eyes were black and handsome, his nose quite large but well shaped. All this Marco noted as he stood before the Khan.

The Khan continued speaking. He turned to the elder Polos and asked: "Where are the hundred men of learning which I desired?"

It was then that Marco's father and uncle stepped forward to explain exactly what had happened. They told the Khan everything. They explained why they had been so long delayed and how they finally saw the new pope. They told about the two frightened friars. And they said that they had with them letters and presents which the Pope had sent.

The presents were then brought into the palace hall and unwrapped. They were placed on the steps before the throne. The letters were translated and read. But the Khan was not pleased. He was disappointed in the letters and little impressed by the presents. All this was a poor substitute for the hundred scholars which he had hoped to receive from Europe. For the Khan felt that the glory of a land does not rest with gold or silver, but rather with learning. Learning, he held, leads to understanding and understanding brings enlightenment.

And so he waved his hand and had the presents from the Pope removed from his sight. He was disappointed, yet he did not blame the Polos for the failure of their mission. He made this clear and in a hundred ways he proved to them that they were welcome. He even sent for robes of honour which he presented to them. And he made them put on these fine robes in his presence.

"And now that you are safely returned to my court, here you will remain," he said. "And never again will I send you on so long and so perilous a journey."

The Khan could see that the travellers were weary from their long journey and he did not unduly prolong his audience with them. He commanded that they be given special rooms in the palace and that the royal cooks should prepare for them whatever dishes they liked best. He urged the Polos to rest and said that he would look forward to seeing them again very soon.

THE DRUMS OF KUBLAI KHA

CHAPTER IX

PAPER MONEY

EVERYTHING WAS NEW. Everything was different. How was it possible for Marco to rest when there was so much to see?

Leaving his father and uncle behind, he went out at once into the beautiful city of Cambalu with its tiled roofs, its stone towers and its broad paved streets. This was the capital of the vast empire of the Khan. He wandered the streets hour after hour. So many streets and byways! He saw artisans making their wares in open shops. He talked with the people. There was so much to see, so much to learn.

Marco soon learnt that the city of Cambalu was in reality two cities separated by a small river. To the north of the river was the true city of Cambalu which Kublai Khan had built on the ruins of old Peking. But the Khan was one day informed by astrologers that this city planned to rebel against his authority. And so he ordered a new city built on the south side of the river. The new city was called Taidu. And when it was finished the Khan moved all the inhabitants of the old city into the new one. He allowed only those whose loyalty he trusted to remain in old Cambalu. And since the number of his loyal subjects seemed quite large, both cities were well populated.

Marco found that both cities were enclosed by walls. The wall of the old city was made of brick, while the wall of the new city, which formed a perfect square, was made of pounded earth. The width of the base was about ten paces; the width at the top about three paces. And all the battlements were whitewashed. This wall also had twelve gates. In planning this new city the Khan had ordered that all streets should be laid out in squares and that ample room should be allowed for gardens and parks.

In the centre of this new city Marco saw a great bell suspended in a tower. And as he stood admiring it he asked an old man, who happened along, what the purpose of this bell could be.

"Ah," said the old man, "this bell serves a very good purpose. Each night it sounds a curfew. After it has rung its warning tones, no one is allowed on the streets except those on urgent business."

"Do all obey this curfew?" asked Marco.

"Of course," said the old man. "Special guards patrol the streets at night to see that this regulation is obeyed!"

Wandering through the streets of both cities, everything seemed strange and different to Marco. The manners, customs, food, dress, the houses, streets, the teeming crowds, their voices... Here before his eyes was an old world; but for him it was a new world. This was a land as ancient as any, a land rich in tradition. Here was a civilization which had never before been seen and fully recorded by a traveller from Europe.

Marco spent several hours in the colourful bazaars of Cambalu. Here, each day, there arrived caravans with rich merchandise. They came from many parts of the empire. At the different shops and booths, under colourful awnings, one could buy silks, woollens, jewelry made of jade, gold and crystal, as well as rich ornaments, hangings, rugs, brocades, and laces. In other shops were sold fruits, vegetables, meats and all necessary provisions, as well as a hundred different kinds of spices. Then, too, there were places where drugs and herbs were sold, and other places where pots and household wares were offered. Here there were booths where copper and brass were hammered, and close by there were shops where tailors and shoemakers were at work. Almost everything that one desired could be found in the rich bazaars of Cambalu, even slave girls of fair skin and great beauty.

However, the Khan, Marco learnt, was very strict with those who desired unreasonable profit. He had a committee of commercial appraisers to examine all goods and fix the prices at which they might be sold, allowing for a fair profit. The merchants were agreeable to this, for when the public knew that the prices were just, they bought without hesitation. Thus goods were promptly disposed of.

Everything was sold for money. But even the money in Cathay seemed strange to Marco. In the first place there were small brass coins with square holes in the centre. These were called "cash" and were strung on long cords. Then there were silver bars and squares, for many articles were priced in ounces of silver. And the merchants had scales at hand to weigh this silver. There were also some gold coins in circulation. At home, Marco was accustomed to coins of silver and gold. But here in Cathay, he saw a new kind of currency—paper money!

Marco questioned one of the merchants about this currency. "I do not understand why you accept this paper as readily as gold and silver. Certainly paper is not so valuable. In Europe, where I come from, we use only metal coins in trade—copper, silver and gold."

The merchants laughed. He could see that the stranger from a far-off land was much confused and he tried to explain to Marco everything he knew about this paper currency.

"It is very simple," he said. "These paper notes are printed from wood blocks and issued by the Kahn's government. Each note is backed in the treasury by bullion. The value of each note is plainly marked, as you can see, and at any time you can exchange this paper money at the treasury for gold. And when it becomes old and worn, it can also be exchanged for fresh paper money on the payment of a small fee."

"But how do people know that this paper money is genuine?"

"Ah," said the merchant. "Counterfeiting is a serious crime and punishable by death."

Marco carefully examined several paper notes. On the face of each was printed a decorative design of dragons and the value of the note.

Each note was stamped with a vermilion seal.

"That is the vermilion seal of Kublai Khan," said the merchant pointing. "His seal guarantees the value of this currency."

Marco looked closely and read aloud the words stamped in vermilion. "The Seal of Him who upholds the Kingdom and rules the Nations."

"Yes," continued the merchant, "without the Khan's seal this currency would be worthless, but with it this paper money is freely accepted all over Cathay."

Paper money was completely unknown in Europe at that time, and many years later, when Marco returned home from Cathay, no one would believe him when he described this currency. No one could conceive that paper could be made to have the value of silver and gold.

Another curious thing that Marco saw, as he wandered through the streets of the city, was a water clock. It told time in this way: a small tub of water was mounted over a second tub into which, through a bamboo spigot in the upper tub, the water dropped slowly, a single drop at a time. The inside of the bottom tub was marked with lines, and by the level of the water one could read the hour of the day. This curious way to measure time worked perfectly. Marco found these clocks on many of the bridges and other public places in the city. They were placed there for the convenience of the people.

Late that afternoon, before returning home to the palace, Marco climbed the stairs at one of the city gates and stood on top of the city wall. Beneath him, stretching for several miles out toward the country, he saw the crowded suburbs of the great city. Here lived the many thousands who could not find quarters within the city walls. Here, too, were many hotels where visitors and travelling merchants stayed.

In the opposite direction, within the city walls of Taidu, Marco could see in the distance the palace of the great Khan Kublai, mounted like a jewel, in its lovely gardens and green parks.

HE PALACE OF KUBLAI KHAN

CHAPTER X

IN THE PALACE OF KUBLAI KHAN IN CAMBALU

EARLY THE FOLLOWING day Marco was summoned into the Khan's presence. The Khan had been so impressed by his first meeting with the young man that he was eager to talk with him privately. He wanted to hear about the distant places through which the Polos had travelled. He was interested in the people and their manners. He wanted to know how they worked and lived, what they ate and how they played. He wanted to know if they were poor or prosperous. He was curious about minerals, gems and the many articles that were produced in the various lands. A hundred things he wanted to know. All of which Marco was able to answer to the Khan's satisfaction.

Sometimes Marco would consult his notes. Thus he was able to give the Khan the exact names of the places they had passed through and many other accurate details.

During this first interview the time passed quickly for both Marco and the Khan. They had so many interests in common that they enjoyed each other's company. And this meeting marked the beginning of a long friendship.

Before they parted that morning the Khan assigned a guide to Marco. The duty of this guide was to take Marco on a tour of the palace and its surrounding gardens. But so great was the palace, and the park in which it was situated, that it could not all be seen in one day. It was only after several afternoons that Marco had finally seen it all. The great palace built of marble spread out over a large area. It was only one storey high, but in truth this was equivalent to two storeys, so high were the ceilings. The palace was flanked on all sides by wide terraces along the outer edge of which were stone balustrades with carved pillars. Beyond these terraces stretched the palace gardens and park.

The palace itself consisted of many apartments and large halls. Besides the audience chamber, which contained the Khan's throne mounted on a raised dais, there were numerous other chambers used by his state ministers for the business of the empire. There were also, several halls for public functions and banquets.

In one wing was a large apartment used by the Khan himself. In another wing there were halls where tapestries and rugs were woven, rooms for the royal artists and rooms for costumes and embroidery. Here, also, was a hall where one hundred scholars were busy each day translating the classics of Cathay into the Mongolian language. In still another wing there were rooms for the royal astronomers employed by the Khan. And in a stone basement was a laboratory where royal alchemists were busy. They spent their days trying to make gold from base metals and compounding an elixir of life, which would allow a person to live for one hundred years.

With so many chambers and halls and with so many activities all going on at once, the palace was indeed a busy place. And besides the halls of state, royal workrooms and the Khan's private apartment, there were also attached to the palace vast kitchens and quarters for servants and palace guards.

Marco visited all these halls and chambers. And he saw many things which he had never seen before. He asked many questions.

While visiting the throne room Marco noticed a white woollen coat hanging in a special niche beside the throne.

"Whose coat is this?" asked Marco. "And why does it hang here?"

"This simple woollen coat," explained the guide, "once belonged to the Khan's famous grandfather Genghis. And although Genghis conquered most of the world and founded the present dynasty, still he remained to his last days a simple man with simple taste. He did not care for the luxuries of life. And this coat was his only coat."

Marco was curious and he examined the coat carefully. It was indeed a simple coat. It was made of ordinary homespun wool.

The guide continued. "This coat is now held sacred by the Mongolians. And it has been placed here beside the throne so that when a subject bows before the Khan he is also bowing before the memory of Genghis, founder of the dynasty."

Marco could not help noticing the contrast presented by the simplicity of the grandfather's coat and the great luxuries surrounding the grandson Kublai. But these thoughts he kept to himself as he and the guide left the the room.

Behind the palace Marco was shown several large buildings. These buildings contained the private property of the Khan, such as his gold and silver bullion, precious stones and pearls and his vessels of gold and silver.

Not far from these buildings was another group of buildings which contained the apartments of his wives and concubines. The guide explained to Marco that the Khan had four wives of the first rank, as well as innumerable concubines. Each one of his four wives bore the title of empress. And the eldest son born of any of these might succeed to the throne.

His concubines were women of exceptional beauty. And the guide explained that they were chosen in the following manner.

"The Khan has special commissioners who are experts in the appraisal of feminine beauty," he said. "And it is the duty of these commissioners to journey to all parts of Cathay to select for the Khan's palace the most beautiful girls in the whole land."

This seemed a most curious custom to Marco, for in Europe such a practice was unknown. He urged the guide to tell him more.

"These commissioners are sometimes able to bring to Cambalu a hundred beautiful girls in a single year," said the guide. "But often

THE WIVES OF KUBLAI KHAN

they do not find so many. You see, their standards are high. They are extremely critical, and even in the greatest beauties they find some defects."

"By what standards is a girl judged fitting to be brought to the court?" asked Marco.

"Ah, the commissioners have a system of rating beauty in which they give points for special features," replied the guide. "A certain number of points are given for the hair, the curve of the lips, the symmetry of the body, grace, the eyes, the arch of the eyebrows and other feature. These points are then added together and only those girls who attain a high score are brought to the palace in Cambalu."

"Do not the parents object to having their daughters taken from them?" asked Marco.

"Of course not. The parents consider it a great honour to have a daughter at court. And the parents also know that in the palace their daughter will be well cared for and that she may some day perhaps marry a prince, a minister of state or some other high-ranking officer."

The guide then explained that when these beautiful girls arrived at the palace they were placed in charge of matrons and tutors. They were given royal gowns and instructed in the etiquette of the court. Those who displayed special talents were given lessons in music, dancing, embroidery, painting or writing.

When the period of training had ended, the girls were divided into groups of five. These groups attended the Khan in his private chambers. Each group served in his apartment for three days, then another group would take its place. During the entire year these groups rotated one after another.

The guide further explained that the Khan would sometimes select one of his beautiful girls and, with her consent, present her as a bride to some foreign prince or faithful minister.

"When one of the Khan's beautiful girls is selected to become a bride," said the guide, "then there is a great buzz of excitement throughout the palace. Special costumes are designed for her. She is showered with presents. And the Khan fills her chest with costly furs, silks, jade, crystal, gold and silver ornaments and even carved ivories and rare porcelains. No princess of any land receives a finer dowry!"

The guide now took Marco through the gardens and parks about the palace. Here he saw many beautiful trees and rolling lawns and meadows. Grazing in these meadows were tame deer, gazelles and other peaceful animals. He saw peacocks and a great variety of beautiful wild birds. The lakes and streams of this park were stocked with fish. Carved stone bridges of great beauty spanned the streams. Here and there were fruit trees and flowering shrubs and garden pagodas made of lacquered bamboo trimmed with beaten gold and silver.

At the far end of the park there was another palace, smaller in size than the palace of the Khan but equally beautiful. "Here lives the Khan's eldest son Chinkin," said the guide. "He is heir to the throne. He is the eldest son of the Khan's twenty-two sons by his four wives."

Close by this second palace was a great mound known as the Green Mount. In the centre of this mount stood a lovely green pagoda surrounded by many beautiful and unusual evergreen trees. Marco was much impressed by the beauty of the Green Mount and he stood a long time admiring it.

"The Kahn loves these trees," explained the guide. "Whenever he hears of an unusually rare specimen he orders that it should be carefully dug up, brought to Cambalu and planted here."

Then the guide pointed to some buildings and a great meadow behind the Green Mount. "Those are the Khan's stables," he said. "In those stables are stalls for the Khan's thousand white horses."

"A thousand white horses!"

"Yes, a thousand horses. Those white horses are sacred. They are carefully cared for and are used for breeding the many horses needed by the Khan's armies." The guide was silent for a moment and then he added: "The mares are milked and from this milk is made a clotted kumiss. I do not myself like the taste of this kumiss but the Khan and his court enjoy it greatly. They consider it a delicacy."

The guide now led Marco on.

The palace and gardens of the Khan were enclosed by two great walls, one set within the other. The outer wall separated the Khan's property from the city itself. The inner wall enclosed and protected the Khan's palace and gardens.

In the space between these two walls were stationed the Khan's troops and their military stores. There were special armouries for these stores. The bridles, saddles, stirrups and other equipment of the cavalry filled one storehouse. The bows, strings, quivers, arrows and other articles of archery occupied another building. Breastplates and other armour formed of hardened leather occupied a third storehouse, and so on for all the different branches requiring military equipment.

While these walls were ruled over by the Khan's soldiers the Khan himself and his great palace were protected by a special bodyguard. This bodyguard was made up of large men, some almost giants. And Marco was greatly surprised to discover that these men were all Christians. He was curious to know where they had come from and why the Khan had chosen them as his personal bodyguard.

"These Christians," said the guide, "are descendants of captives taken by Genghis. Their parents were born in distant lands, in lands near the Caucasian Mountains."

"Oh, I know where those lands are!" said Marco. "We travelled near them on our journey from Europe."

"Then you must know about these Christians. Some belong to Greek church and some are called Nestorian Christians."

Marco, of course, knew about the Greek church in Asia Minor and he had spoken with Nestorian's in western Cathay.

"But tell me," he asked, "why the Khan employs Christians for his bodyguard."

The guide spoke confidently. "You see there is great rivalry in the palace between the Mongols and the Chinese and the Khan very wisely wants a bodyguard of a race apart, a group that does not mix easily with others. Such a group, he feels, will not readily fall in with palace intrigues." Then he laughed. "Do you know what the Khan calls these Christians?"

"No," said Marco.

"Well, he calls them 'the luminous ones' because at the mention of their Lord their faces glow with ecstasy! They are very ardent believers."

All these things Marco learnt during his early days in the palace of Kublai Khan in Cambalu.

CHAPTER XI

A PATRON OF THE ARTS

IN THE DAYS that followed, Marco and the Khan spent many pleasant hours together. They talked of all kinds of things which interested them. The Khan wanted to know about life in Europe and how it differed from life in Cathay. He was extremely interested in the differences which Marco pointed out to him.

And he asked Marco what one thing in Cathay he considered most unusual. Marco thought for a time, then he answered: "Religious freedom".

The Khan was surprised at this answer for he thought that surely in Europe they must enjoy great religious tolerance. And after Marco had explained to the Khan that this was not so, the Khan expressed his views on this subject.

"It is a principle of mine never to interfere with the religion of any sect in my empire. I treat all equally. In fact I protect all religions and allow no intolerance of one religious group against another. As a matter of fact, I believe that people should worship whatever gods they like."

Marco was most interested in the words of the Khan. He was eager to hear more.

The Khan went on to say that he himself was very doubtful about the power of gods. He said that he often asked his devout subjects to demonstrate to him the power of their gods. The best gods after all, he reasoned, were those who listened to the prayers of their worshippers and granted the favours asked of them. Gods who turned a deaf ear he deemed as false and unworthy. He said he was ever sceptical, yet willing to be convinced and, above all, he was tolerant of other people's right to believe.

The Khan continued. "Religious freedom existed in Cathay long before my illustrious grandfather conquered the land. In those days, just as you see it now, there were Buddhists, Mohammedans, Idolaters, Christians and Jews, worshipping and living side by side in peace. Many of these people inter-married as they do to-day. At this very time in my court there are Tartar princes married to Christians."

Marco was surprised to hear the Khan's words. He did not know that there were Jews in Cathay and he wanted to hear about them.

"As early as the seventh century," the Khan said, "large numbers of Jews, having fled from Arabia and Persia, where they were persecuted by the Mohammedans, found refuge in Cathay. Here in Cathay they have lived in peace for many centuries. And, to-day, they still enjoy peace and worship freely in their synagogues. We call them the ancestors of Adam, the first man. And recently when one of their synagogues was destroyed by fire I rebuilt it for them at my own expense. As a matter of fact, my personal doctor, a man of great learning and culture, is a Jew."

The Khan repeated again that he believed in religious freedom. He said that intolerance is a bad thing, a product of ignorance. Those who practise intolerance, he warned, often live to feel intolerance practised against them.

The Khan was silent for a brief moment, then he smiled in a friendly way: "It matters not," he said, "what gods my subjects worship. On my birthday, as you will see for yourself, all in Cathay pray for my health and prosperity."

And Marco was soon to find that this was true.

The great Khan Kublai's birthday was on the twenty eighth day of September. Long before this day arrived, ambassadors, princes of the realm and envoys began gathering in Cambalu. They came from all parts of the Orient with gifts for the Khan. There were chieftains of distant Mongolian tribes and princes of lands owing allegiance. Some brought bars of gold and others brought jewels, vases of jade, rock crystal and other precious ornaments. Some from the Far North, which is now called Siberia, brought pelts of rare sables and ermine.

But there were many, also, who used this occasion to present petitions to the Khan asking for special favours. Some wanted to be appointed governors of cities; some desired elevation in rank or title. Some asked for positions as tax collectors or other profitable occupations. There were, in fact, so many who arrived each year with petitions that the Khan appointed a committee of twelve barons to receive these requests and sift out those that seemed reasonable and worthy.

At length, when the twenty-eighth day of September arrived, in all the places of worship in his dominions—in churches, synagogues, mosques and temples—incense was burnt and candles were lighted. And the name of Kublai was praised to the heavens. All who owed allegiance to the Khan paid homage on this, the day of his birth.

In the afternoon of this day a great birthday feast was given in the banquet hall of the palace in Cambalu. Here in this long hall, and on this occasion, Marco and the elder Polos found themselves among the honoured guests, at a table with foreign princes.

Marco noticed that at this banquet the seating arrangement was most unusual. The Khan sat at a small elevated table facing the length of the room. Next to him on his left-hand side sat one of his four wives. At a table to his right sat his sons, grandsons and others related to him by blood. This table was somewhat lower than the table at which the Khan sat. Other princes and nobles had places at still lower tables. And the same was true for the wives of the sons, grandsons and for the other ladies of the court who were all seated at the Khan's left-hand side. Then there were tables for the wives of ministers and military officers. All were seated according to their respective ranks and dignities.

However, all those who had come to celebrate the Khan's birthday

HE WHITE FEAST

could not be accommodated in the main hall. The greater number of the guests ate while sitting on carpets in some of the adjacent rooms.

For this great occasion the Khan was dressed in his finest robes, all woven of threads of pure gold. He wore his state jewels and a belt of gold. His relatives and guests were also dressed in costly robes made of silk with belts of gold and silver. Most of these beautiful robes had been presented to them by the Khan himself. And the costumes of those whom the Khan held in high esteem were embellished with real pearls and other jewels. Marco estimated that some of these robes had the value of ten thousand pieces of gold each. Never in his life had he seen a more dazzling sight.

After all had found their places, the stewards and their assistants brought in great numbers of dishes for the guests. Such a variety of things to eat Marco had never dreamed possible. The Khan, however, was served by some of his barons, all of whom had their noses and mouths covered by fine handkerchiefs so that his food and wine might not be affected by their breath.

Each time that the Khan called for a drink—and after the goblet had been handed to him—those who were serving him and all the guests in the hall knelt on the floor and bowed low in reverence. At the same time the musicians began to play. This continued until the Khan finished drinking. Then all the company rose again and returned to the feast. And as often as the Khan drank, this ceremony was repeated!

As soon as the feast was over, at a given signal from the Khan, jugglers, tumblers and other entertainers entered the hall and began to display their feats. Then, when these finished performing, their places were taken by dancers and musicians. Finally, the Khan sent for his Yellow Lamas. These dark priests who wore great yellow turbans claimed that they could control the weather, producing rain or sunshine at will. They also claimed other supernatural powers. In fact all of their tricks of magic, they said, were produced through the supernatural. And, since they were anxious for the Khan to believe that they had these wonderful powers, they would never disclose to anyone how their tricks of magic were done.

On this day as soon as they entered the hall they approached the Khan's table and, striking dramatic attitudes, they asked the Khan to hold out his hand. Then, in sight of all, they caused a golden goblet to rise, travel slowly through the air and come to rest in his outstretched hand. After the Khan had drunk from the golden goblet, they caused the wine pitcher to travel unaided through the air and pour some fresh wine into the Khan's goblet. When this was done, the pitcher floated slowly back to its place of rest. This feat of magic they did for the amusement of the Khan and his guests.

These Yellow Lamas were masters of the art of mystification and illusion. And at a later time, when Marco travelled through Cathay on behalf of the Khan, he often stayed overnight at monasteries belonging to these lamas. He was ever entertained by their feats of magic. But he soon learnt that the Red Lamas of Cathay, a rival sect, regarded their Yellow brethren with great contempt. They called them unorthodox and said that they were only cheap tricksters and charlatans. Nevertheless, these Yellow Lamas were able to perform many wonderful magical tricks which even to this day have not been repeated by our famous magicians.

However, it was at the Khan's birthday banquet that Marco first saw a performance put on by the Yellow Lamas. The illusions they created on this occasion were indeed entertaining as well as mystifying. And there were many present who were truly convinced that these holy men had supernatural powers.

When the Yellow Lamas had finished displaying their feats of magic the banquet was over. The guests then rose and departed for home.

Another festival which was celebrated by all in Cathay was the White Feast or New Year's Day. This day was the greatest holiday of the year and on this day the Khan again received gifts and gave a banquet.

But for this day the Khan and his guests did not dress in gold and colourful silks. Instead they dressed in robes of white for white was considered an emblem of good fortune. And throughout Cathay on this day the people, also, according to their means, wore something white to bring good fortune in the new year. It was a day of festivity everywhere and the people embraced each other saying: "May good fortune attend you through the coming year, and may everything you undertake succeed to your wish."

It was on this day, too, that the Khan paraded his royal elephants—of which he had several thousand—through the streets of Cambalu. The elephants were gaily decorated with rich rugs and mounted with colourful howdahs, in which rode members of the court. All was gay and festive.

Within the palace all the princes of the land, nobles of various rank and members of the Khan's household assembled in a great hall. When all were in their places, a noble of high rank rose and said in a loud voice: "Bow down and do reverence!" Instantly all knelt and touched their foreheads to the floor. This was repeated four times. Then the noble advanced to an altar upon which stood a red tablet inscribed with the name of the great Khan. And with burning incense he perfumed both the tablet and the altar. As he did so, all present humbly prostrated themselves with great reverence.

When this ceremony was concluded a feast was given, after which there was a theatrical performance by the members of the Khan's Imperial Theatre. When the play was over everyone returned to his own home.

Marco was to discover, among many other things, that the Khan was the first emperor of Cathay to encourage the development of the theatre. Before his time, actors were merely wandering minstrels. And it was the Khan Kublai who brought together the best actors in Cambalu and gave them money to establish the first Imperial Theatre of Cathay.

Besides helping actors, the Khan supported the famous poets of the land, as well as playwrights and novelists. He had great respect for writers, artists and actors. He gave them what they required to live so that they were free to devote all their time to their art. Many works of literature and many wonderful paintings done in the time of the Khan have survived to this very day and are still much admired. And but for the Khan's royal patronage they might never have been created.

After all the savage accounts which Marco had heard about the Mongolians when he lived in Europe, he was puzzled, here at the royal court, to find such a high degree of culture. How was it possible that the grandson of the savage Genghis Khan could be a man so well educated and enlightened? The answer was simple.

While the Mongolians were a primitive and ignorant people, the Chinese, whom they conquered, were not. When Genghis overran the land, the people of Cathay already had a culture centuries old. They had wonderful painters, musicians, poets, novelists and sculptors. They had already developed the art of printing, which was unknown in the rest of the world. They had great knowledge of agriculture, medicine, mathematics, astronomy, engineering and architecture. They made the most beautiful porcelains in the world. And their cooking had been developed to a high art. These were only a few of their accomplishments. Their entire mode of life was one of refinement and culture, supported by a philosophy.

It was into this cultured world that the barbaric Mongolians came. They were surrounded by the culture of Cathay and they could not help but absorb it. They soon made themselves part of the life around them. They not only became part of the old culture but soon they championed it.

CHAPTER XII

SPRING HUNTING

IT WAS THE custom of the Khan to spend six months in Cambalu, three spring months on the great hunt and the summer months—June, July and August—in Xanadu.

In the month of February, as soon as the New Year's celebration was done, the Khan prepared for the spring hunt. After six winter months in the palace of Cambalu the Khan grew restless. And so each year in the early spring he and his retinue would leave on a hunting trip.

Marco Polo was able to describe these hunts in great detail because he was often invited to accompany the Khan.

Each year, on the first day of March, the Khan and his party left the city of Cambalu. They usually made their way toward the ocean, for the country there was wooded and abounded in all kinds of wild game.

The hunting party consisted of thousands of people—guests, women of the court, masters of the hunt, soldiers and servants.

A long wagon train carrying tents, provisions and everything else that was necessary for the comfort of the Khan and his guests, started out first. Arriving at the place where the hunt was to be held, numerous camps were set up in different locations. This was done so that the hunters were distributed over a wide territory. The Khan's camp naturally was the largest.

Some hours after the provision train had departed, the royal hunting party left Cambalu. The Khan rode on a great elephant. In the howdah, lined with cloth of gold and covered on the outside with tiger skins, the Khan reclined on a couch. The princes and other royal guests rode on fine horses. The ladies of the court were carried in palanquins, and all were attended by hundreds of servants and guarded over by selected companies of soldiers.

With this party travelled special huntsmen who were expert handlers of hounds. There were also hundreds of falconers who had charge of the hunting falcons, hawks and eagles. These birds, belonging to the Khan and his guests, had fastened to their legs small silver bands on which were engraved the names of the owners. The Khan also had several trained leopards, lynxes and tigers that at special times were let loose to catch and retrieve forest wildlife. These animals were used in the hunting of boars, wild oxen and asses, bears and stags. They were transported in cages placed upon wagons.

Some of the Khan's favourite ministers and barons took on special duties during the hunt. Thus one baron would have charge of equipment, while another would be master over the thousands of beaters employed by the hunters; still another would be responsible for some other branch of the sport.

One baron, Marco thought, had a very odd job indeed. He was called the "Keeper of Lost Property". If anything were found—a cap, a piece of clothing or a stray falcon—it had to be turned over to this baron. Failure to do so was considered theft and was punishable. It was the duty of this baron to see that all lost property was returned to its proper owners. When the tents were put up, the tent of this baron was placed in a prominent position and marked with distinctive flags so that all could see. In this way, Marco Polo observed, nothing was ever lost but that it was soon restored.

While on the road from Cambalu the Khan liked to proceed at a leisurely pace. In his howdah, on his elephant, he sometimes had a dozen falcons. And for his amusement, from time to time, he let one or two loose to see what birds they could swoop down upon and capture. It afforded the Khan great pleasure, as he lay upon his couch, to watch his falcons overpower cranes or other birds and game.

With such diversions along the road the time went quickly, and

THE HUNT

by evening the Khan and his immediate party made for camp. This camp resembled a city of tents all carefully arranged around the great tent of the Khan.

The Khan's tent was so large that it could accommodate great audiences. Its entrance faced the south and on one side it had another tent connected with it. This smaller tent the Khan used for his private apartment. To the rear of this smaller tent was attached still another tent in which he slept. Near by there were many other tents for the different branches of his household.

The Khan's tents were each secured by silken cords and supported by pillars of spice wood, richly carved and gilded. The exteriors of these tents were covered with tiger skins while the interiors were lined with skins of ermines and sables. Those sable skins were most costly and highly prized by the Mongols. Marco Polo said that a cloak of sable skins was valued at two thousand pieces of gold.

Near the Khan's tent were situated the tents of the court ladies, as well as those of the members of his household such as his physicians and his astronomers.

Some days the Khan and his party hunted along the banks of lakes and rivers. Here they took many storks, swans, herons and other birds. On other days they hunted in the open country with the Khan's trained tigers, lynxes and leopards. And on still other days the Khan's party hunted in the deep forest.

When hunting wild game in the forest, the Khan employed beaters. These men with staves and whistles formed a vast circle, sometimes encompassing an entire mountain. At a given signal they began moving forward, beating the brush with their staves, thus driving all wildlife before them. As they moved forward their circle contracted, making it impossible for any animal to break through. Finally, when the circle had contracted to the space of a single field, and all the wildlife was concentrated in one spot, the hunters arrived. With bows, arrows and spears, the hunters entered this enclosure and killed all the trapped beasts.

In these various ways did the Khan and his guests amuse themselves while on the spring hunt. This lasted a full three months. And when this time was over the entire party returned to Cambalu.

CHAPTER XIII

IN XANADU

> *"Twice five miles of fertile ground*
> *With walls and towers were girdled round"*

IT WAS THE custom of the Khan, after returning from the hunt, to spend only three days in Cambalu. At the end of this time the entire court, together with the Khan's thousand white horses, moved to Xanadu, in the cool Manchurian Hills, to spend the hot summer months.

On the appointed day a great procession was formed. The Khan on a white horse rode at the head. With him, mounted on fine horses, rode his sons, high ministers and generals as well as his court favourites, including the three Polos. Members of his Christian bodyguard flanked this cavalcade.

Next followed the hundreds of palanquins with the empresses and the beautiful ladies of the court. And after these stretched a seemingly endless line of baggage and supply wagons, stewards, servants and other court retainers. The thousand white mares of the Khan, carefully guarded over by special attendants, also rode with this procession.

From Cambalu to Xanadu the road ran in a northerly direction for one hundred and eighteen miles. It pierced the Great Wall which separated Cathay from the rolling Plains of Mongolia.

While the Khan was on his spring hunt crews of labourers, directed by captains and engineers, were sent out to repair this roadway and its many bridges from the ravages brought on by winter frosts. These men also saw that the many rest stations and camping grounds along the way were put into proper condition and ready for the Khan and his royal court.

Several days before the Khan's procession was to start out from Cambalu, crews of palace servants and companies of the Khan's soldiers rode out on this highway. The servants took charge of the camp sites while the soldiers of the Khan took stations all along the way, especially at crossroads. For the royal procession had to be guarded and no one was allowed to enter upon this highway while the Khan and his court were on their journey.

Each day the royal procession trotted along at an easy pace, hour after hour. By late afternoon one of the many royal camp sites was reached and all came to rest for the night. Here they found food and all other provisions already waiting for them. And after resting, the members of the court amused themselves with contests of archery, wrestling and horse racing until nightfall.

Each morning the procession started out again. In this manner, day after day, the court journeyed on toward Xanadu.

When the procession came to the Great Wall of China, which separated the land of Cathay from Mongolia, the Khan called a halt. He then climbed to the top of the great wall and, waiting for all to assemble, poured some sacred mare's milk, from a golden goblet, on the land of Mongolia. As he did this he recited a blessing to his native land. When this sacred rite was over the procession continued on its way. And, at length, after many more days of travelling it reached Xanadu.

In the spring sunlight Xanadu sparkled like a crown of jewels. The Khan had built his beautiful summer palaces on the banks of the blue river Loan. The marshland of the valley had been drained and formed into numerous islands and lakes which were joined by winding waterways and arched stone bridges. The whole valley was made into a vast park with beautiful trees, flowering shrubs and delightful gardens. The landscape was dotted with many colourful pagodas. Their upturned peaked roofs made of coloured glazed tiles sparkled in the sunlight. Pleasure boats floated idly in the lakes and streams where swans, herons, cranes and other water birds lingered.

THE PLEASURE BOAT

Here in Xanadu the Khan built pleasure palaces of marble with broad connecting terraces. There were garden teahouses on long sloping lawns that reached to the river's shore. And set like a gem in all this beauty was the great palace of the Khan. This summer palace was made of polished bamboo, embellished with gold carvings and colourful lacquers. Its many rooms were decorated in vermilion and gold. And some of its walls were beautifully painted with figures, birds, flowers and distant landscapes.

Behind the palaces stretched broad meadows with long stables for the horses and barracks for the soldiers. Here, too, was a race course where the Khan's horses were run for the entertainment of the court.

Once settled on his native Mongolian soil, and breathing the fresh cool air of the hills, the Khan relaxed and felt himself at ease. He was happy. And the mood of the Khan was reflected throughout the entire court. In Xanadu there were less formalities and, for the hot summer months, much of the strict court etiquette was put aside.

Everyone, both men and women, enjoyed themselves. They swam in the pools and often rode out into the surrounding hills. They went on picnics and played many games.

Indoors they were entertained by jugglers, dancers, musicians, comedians and those Yellow Lamas who created mystifying illusions. Then, toward the end of the summer a troupe of actors from the Khan's Imperial Theatre would arrive in Xanadu. Each year new plays as well as old favourites were presented.

When the three hot summer months were over, the Khan chose a day for the court to start the return journey to the city of Cambalu. By the end of the summer the Khan had had enough pleasure and was ready to return to take up the business of ruling his large empire. And so every year, in the last week of August, the long royal procession started back over the highway that joined Xanadu with Cambalu.

It is not possible to speak of Xanadu without recording a happening that took place in England five centuries after Marco Polo had visited this pleasure city. After reading Marco Polo's adventures, the famous poet Coleridge, fascinated by Xanadu, dreamed one night about the pleasure palaces of the Khan. When he awoke he wrote out what he had seen in his dream. This poem, entitled Kubla Khan, he was unable to finish. But the fragment which he managed to capture from the dream is recognized to-day as one of the great poems of the world.

Here are the magical lines, which begin this famous unfinished poem, inspired by Marco Polo.

> In Xanadu did Kubla Khan
> A stately pleasure-dome decree:
> Where Alph, the sacred river, ran
> Through caverns measureless to man
> Down to a sunless sea.
> So twice five miles of fertile ground
> With walls and towers were girdled round:
> And there were gardens bright with sinuous rills
> Where blossom'd many an incense-bearing tree;
> And here were forests ancient as the hills,
> Enfolding sunny spots of greenery.

It is a great loss to literature that this poem remains unfinished. And it is a great loss to the world that to-day little trace of Xanadu can be found. What has happened to this paradise built by Kublai?

Alas! All has crumbled to ruin. Even the name, Xanadu, is hard to find on a map because the Chinese of to-day call this place Shangtu.

It is now a deserted, lonely site, overgrown with rank weeds and grass. The valley has returned to swampland. And, on the long slope where the gorgeous palaces of the Khan once stood, now only rock and rubble can be seen. Here and there the outlines of some of the foundation walls can be traced in the ruins. Scattered over the ground are fallen blocks of white marble, pieces of stone lions, carved dragons and other sculptured fragments. This is all that remains of the former glory of Xanadu.

Time and neglect have brought dust and ruin to what was once a city of splendour.

CHAPTER XIV

MARCO POLO SPEAKS OUT

RETURNING FROM XANADU one autumn, Marco found the city of Cambalu under martial law. One of the Khan's high ministers, whose name was Achmath, had just been assassinated. Soldiers patrolled the streets and everyone under suspicion was arrested.

The Khan was upset. Achmath had been one of his favourites and he immediately appointed judges to try all involved in the assassination.

The Khan, however, did not know that Achmath was in truth a very dishonest man. He had been the leader of a group of public officials who had grown rich through extortion and misappropriation.

Through the years Achmath had gained great power over the Khan through flattery and falsehood. He always appeared to be devoting his entire life to the service of the Khan, when in reality he was only serving his own interests.

In time his power over the Khan became so great that in the summer he stayed behind in Cambalu and acted as governor. The Khan also gave him the privilege of distributing government positions. These, of course, he gave to friends and colleagues. Many of them became governors and they were usually corrupt. For each appointment Achmath received, privately, a sum of money. In time he amassed a great fortune and owned a fine home on one of the broad avenues of Cambalu. He explained his wealth by saying that his wife inherited vast properties from her father and uncles.

Now if anyone dared to protest, Achmath would go to the Khan and say: "so-and-so has committed an offence against your dignity and deserves death". And the Khan, trusting Achmath, would say: "do with so-and-so as you think right." Thus Achmath was able to get rid of his enemies. In this way he also intimidated everyone, and in time no one dared to oppose him in anything. No one was so high in rank or power as to be free from the dread of him.

But now he himself had been beheaded by an assassin. And Marco Polo was ordered by the Khan to investigate all rumours connected with this plot. He was to find out why this deed had been accomplished.

Accordingly, Marco went to the palace dungeon and spoke with the assassin Chenchu. This man Chenchu was a high Chinese military officer. From his lips Marco heard why the assassination was planned and how it was carried out.

Chenchu told Marco how he and another Chinese officer named Vanchu had decided that Achmath was responsible for too much unhappiness in the land of Cathay. And because of this they decided that he must die. They communicated their intention to prominent citizens in all parts of the land. Many joined willingly in this plot. Achmath's assassination was to set off a general revolt against the Mongolian conquerors. The governors of all the cities of Cathay were to be destroyed.

"The Khan does not know how oppressed are the people of Cathay," said Chenchu. "You see, the great Khan is a good ruler, but he has not succeeded to the throne of Cathay by hereditary right. He holds his power through conquest. We are a conquered people. And the Khan does not have confidence in us. He therefore puts all government authority into the hands of Mongolians, Mohammedans and Christians. Most of these men have been appointed by the tyrant Achmath. We people of Cathay consider these men foreigners and we do not like to be ruled by them. Often they treat us like slaves. And the worst tyrant of all was Achmath."

Then Chenchu told an endless tale of the abuses that Achmath and his friends had practiced against the people. And finally he related to Marco how he and Vanchu, after entering the palace rooms, sent a messenger to the home of the corrupt minister Achmath, to say that the Crown Prince Chinkin, eldest son of the Khan, had just returned to Cambalu and desired to see him without delay. This, of course, was a lie.

In the meantime Vanchu put on a royal robe and pretended he was Chinkin. After lighting many tallow candles he sat waiting for the minister. Chenchu hid close by, armed with a great sword.

Now when Achmath passed through the gates in the palace walls the captain of the guard grew suspicious.

"Where are you bound for at this late hour?" he asked.

"To the Crown Prince Chinkin, who has just arrived," replied the minister.

"How can that be?" said the captain of the guard. "I did not hear of his arrival. And such things I should know. I had better go along with you."

With a few soldiers he followed a short distance behind Achmath.

"As Achmath entered the chamber," explained Chenchu, "he saw many candles burning. He naturally thought that the Crown Prince had arrived, for who else would be so extravagant? And although he could not see his face he immediately bowed down before the robed figure. When he did so, I came out of hiding, quickly drew my sword and struck off his head. Now at this very moment the captain and his soldiers entered the room. Seeing the head roll to the floor and recognizing Vanchu dressed in royal robes, the captain sent a swift arrow to his heart. Vanchu fell dead. In the meantime the soldiers overpowered me and made me prisoner. That is exactly what happened," concluded Chenchu.

"And the other cities of Cathay, why did they not revolt against their governors?" asked Marco.

"Had we been fully successful they would have been encouraged. But with Vanchu shot dead, myself arrested and charged with treason and martial law declared in the city of Cambalu, they had no spirit to rise... I now await my end. What I have done I have done for the people of Cathay."

After Marco Polo had heard this story and collected as much information about this attempted revolt as he could, he went to the Khan. He spoke out boldly, although he knew that his words against the late minister Achmath would certainly not please the Khan.

He told the Khan exactly what he had learned about the corruption of Achmath and how for twenty-two years he had perpetrated endless outrages against the people of the land. He told the Khan how he sold political offices and how he received commissions from all tax collectors. "All his wealth came from dishonesties," Marco said. "Call in his sons and have them examined; then you will know that I speak the truth."

The sons were brought before the Khan and they readily confessed that their father had gained his wealth by dishonest methods. Since these sons also confessed that they had aided their father in demanding graft and extortion, the Khan ordered that they should be beaten with canes. When this was done he further ordered that the entire treasure amassed by his minister be confiscated.

As for the captain Chenchu, and the others who were implicated in this plot, they were ordered to be beheaded.

The Khan considered everything that Marco Polo related and he took steps to see that justice was done. He removed the friends of Achmath from office and appointed new governors who were instructed to rule justly and within the limits of the law.

When this whole affair was concluded the Khan called Marco Polo before the throne, and in the presence of all his ministers he complimented him on his courage to speak the truth. He then appointed him assessor of the privy council. In the presence of all assembled he gave him the robes of this high office and a golden tablet of authority.

And Marco bowed low four times when he accepted these gifts and swore his allegiance to the Khan.

CHAPTER XV

PRINTING, ICE-CHARCOAL AND ASTROLOGERS

As a high-ranking officer of the Khan's privy council, Marco learned about the organization of the government.

To carry the burden of government the Khan had created two high tribunals. One was a military body called the Thai. The other body, which ruled civilian affairs, was called the Sing. Each tribunal had a building of its own.

The Thai tribunal was the supreme military body of the land and was responsible only to the Khan. It consisted of twelve high-ranking noblemen who had authority over all military matters. They approved of troop movements and made the plans for all military campaigns.

The Sing tribunal had charge of all the internal affairs of the thirty-four provinces of the land. This tribunal also consisted of twelve men. It was often called the second tribunal because it was not considered as important as the military tribunal.

In the Sing building each province of the land had a separate wing of offices. Here, too, were the departments of taxation, justice, highways, commerce and currency.

But Marco Polo was not only interested in the organization of the Khan's government, he was also interested in the people which he saw in and around Cambalu. He was curious about how they lived and how they worked. Here he found many things which were different or unknown in Europe.

Among other things, Marco saw in Cambalu how printing was

done with movable type. This craft was not known in Europe until two hundred years later. He also saw another thing which he considered most amazing. The people used black stones for fuel instead of wood! This stone, mined in the hills, was brought into the city. And Marco noted that it burned like charcoal and was much better than wood, for it easily sustained its fire until morning. He also noted that it gave out a great deal of heat. Although in Europe, at that time, coal was completely unknown, in Cathay it had been used for fuel since ancient times. It was called "ice charcoal".

Marco was told that throughout the land of Cathay the people believed in astrology. They believed that the stars in the sky influenced human affairs and even predicted future events. According to the position of the heavenly bodies one could predict which days were lucky and which days unlucky.

In Cambalu alone, Marco noted that there were about five thousand astrologers whose food and clothing the emperor provided. They spent their days studying charts of the heavens and predicting events to come. They foretold the weather, plagues, wars, discords and conspiracies as well as fortunate events. In the streets and market places these astrologers sold cards of predictions for a copper each. And the people, believing in them, bought freely.

Anyone wanting to undertake a long journey or engage in a new venture would first consult an astrologer. This astrologer, after studying the position of the stars at the hour of the person's birth, would predict all the good and bad fortune that might befall his client. And the person so instructed would not dare go against the astrologer's advice.

So strong are the roots of this belief that even to this very day the Chinese consult their astrologers. And their printed almanac—which is found in almost every home—has the unlucky days of the year marked in black letters. On such days everything is done with great caution.

But besides the astrologers, Marco Polo also saw another group

THE OBSERVATORY OF PEKIN

of men who were greatly concerned with the heavens. These men employed by the Khan were astronomers. They were men of science and did not believe in fortune telling.

The Khan employed the best astronomers he was able to find. Some of these scholars he brought from Persia and other far countries. They designed wonderful astronomical instruments which the Khan had cast in bronze and mounted on the terraces of his palace. By means of these instruments, the Khan's astronomers were truly able to foretell an eclipse of the sun or moon. They had names for many of the planets and stars. And they spent long days drawing charts of the heavens, making mathematical calculations and revising the Chinese calendar.

The years in China, Marco discovered, were divided into cycles. A cycle consisted of twelve years and these years were named as follows: one Rat, two Ox, three Tiger, four Hare, five Dragon, six Serpent, seven Horse, eight Sheep, nine Ape, ten Cock, eleven Dog, twelve Swine. When the cycle of twelve was ended, a new cycle started again from the beginning. Thus the Chinese might say: "It was the year of the ox when the house burnt down", or "My first son was born in the year of the Dragon my second son was born in the year of the Dog."

To this very day the years in China are marked by the names of the years in the cycle of twelve.

Time has crumbled the walls of the palace of Kublai Khan, but the beautiful bronze astronomical instruments, which Marco saw centuries ago on the terraces in Cambalu, are well preserved. They stand to-day as a monument to an old culture and as evidence of Marco Polo's truthfulness.

CHAPTER XVI

MISSION TO TIBET

ONE DAY, AFTER Marco had served in the privy council for several years, the Khan spoke with him privately.

"I would like you to undertake a long trip for me to the border of Tibet and into the southern provinces. I want an accurate report of these areas. It has been some years since I have sent a personal representative through these districts, and I am interested in knowing about the changing social conditions, how the people in these distant parts regard my rule, how they prosper and what problems they face. I also want a complete report on all industries, their profits and losses and the possibilities of further taxation."

The Khan chose Marco as his emissary because he felt that Marco showed an unusual talent for observation of people and conditions of life. Since Marco was a European everything in the Orient was unnaturally strange and interesting to him. He therefore noticed many things which a native of Cathay would have taken for granted.

Marco was very pleased to be so honoured by the Khan. He knew that there were many in the court who were very able and who might have been chosen by the Khan in his stead. It was therefore very gratifying for him to know that the Khan held him in such high regard.

He immediately began making preparations for the journey, and at the end of a week he was ready to leave Cambalu. He said good-bye to his father and uncle who were now, with the Khan's permission, busily engaged in trade. They still lived in the palace but they owned a large warehouse in Cambalu and conducted a business in imports and exports.

After the Khan had invested Marco with a golden tablet of authority and given him a list of the places he desired him to visit, Marco set out on his mission. He was now a special ambassador of the Khan's and could demand the best horses and all else that he required at the posthouses along the way. He was dressed in the robes of his office and wherever he went he was shown great respect.

He had not travelled farther than thirty Chinese li—which is the equivalent of ten miles—when he arrived at the Pulisangan River.

Across this river was a stone bridge such as Marco, in all his travels, had never seen before. It was built of fine white marble, and beneath its twenty-four arches there were many water mills which used the swift current of the river to grind grain. The bridge was so wide that ten horsemen could ride abreast. Along the stone railings of the bridge were ornamental columns with carved lions. It was not only a marvel of engineering but also a work of great beauty.

On the road westward, Marco passed through many great cities and he met with merchants who travelled to India and other far-off places. He crossed rivers and mountains and visited the great castles of the land.

It was in the western part of Cathay that Marco Polo first came to the great Yellow River. He said that it was so wide and deep that no bridge could ever be erected across it. He noted that on its banks were many towns, in which there were castles where merchants resided. And he said that it served as an important traffic lane. Many inland merchants sent their boats of cargo down this waterway to the coast of Cathay and into the Yellow Sea.

In one province Marco stayed at a palace which had been built by a king of long ago. Here in the great hall he saw beautiful scroll paintings of all the ancient kings of this land. Each had a history, each a legend. Of one of these rulers, who was called the Golden King, Marco heard the following story.

The Golden King was envied and hated by the king of a neighbouring country. This neighbour determined to capture him. Accord-

THE BRIDGE OF PULISANGE

ingly, he sent to the palace of the Golden King fifteen cavaliers who presented themselves, saying that they had come from some distant land, and offered their services. The Golden King, not suspecting evil, welcomed these strangers. Through the months that followed, the cavaliers served him diligently and ably so that they thus gained his esteem.

Now one day when the Golden King was engaged in hunting he crossed a river, separating himself from his own people. The cavaliers, who were with him, quickly drew their swords, surrounded him and led him away to their real king.

The Golden King, now a prisoner, was clothed in rags and humiliated by being sent out to tend cattle. He did the work of a herdsman without complaint. This fortitude impressed his captor so much that at the end of two years he released the Golden King and let him return to his people. From that time on these neighbouring kings were friends.

Leaving the palace of the Golden King, Marco travelled on. In some districts he found that the people engaged in industries, while in other places they worked the land and devoted their lives to agriculture. In one district, where mulberry trees grew, he found that the people raised cocoons. They spun silk thread and wove beautiful cloth. And wherever he went—through valleys, over mountains and even through deep forests—Marco found the Khan's posthouses.

In populated sections these posthouses were spaced twenty-five to thirty miles apart. In open country they were spaced much farther apart. But no matter how remote the district, there was always at least one posthouse. And at each posthouse there was a stable of the Khan's horses for his ambassadors and his couriers. Marco Polo estimated that many thousands of horses were used in this service, and that throughout the land there were at least ten thousand posthouses. Everywhere these houses were filled with travellers. There were many travellers on the roads of Cathay, for the roads were patrolled by the Khan's soldiers and travelling was safe. Highwaymen did not dare engage in robbery.

Now, as Marco went farther west, the land became more mountainous. Here there were all kinds of wild beasts, especially lions and bears. And they were so numerous that one was in constant danger.

The natives told all travellers who were forced to sleep out at night how to keep the wild beasts at a distance.

"Build a great bonfire," they said. "And then throw into the flames some large stalks of green bamboo. The sap of the fresh bamboo will soon begin to boil and steam. And the steam trapped between the sealed joints of the bamboo will create so great a pressure that the bamboo will explode with a terrific noise. These explosions will frighten off any prowling beasts."

"However," the natives warned, "be sure to have your horses tied to trees and their legs firmly shackled, for when the explosions occur they, too, will be greatly frightened. Horses have been known to run off, leaving their masters stranded!"

Here in this wild country Marco found a savage people. Their tribe was completely cut off from the cultured areas of Cathay. The members of the tribe lived almost entirely on the wild game they shot with bows and arrows. They dressed in the skins of animals. And to help them hunt wild beasts, they had dogs of a very special breed—as large as mastiffs.

Among the rare animals that these savages hunted was the famous musk deer. They collected the valuable musk, which they gave to traders in exchange for salt.

These savages on the borderland of Tibet had no use for the Khan's paper money. However, since salt was rare in these mountains and therefore valuable, they used pressed cakes of salt as currency. These cakes of salt served two purposes: they were used as money and also, when needed, to flavour food.

While travelling through this strange part of the world, Marco spent many nights in the monasteries of the Yellow Lamas. The country abounded in monasteries of this order. And while Marco was with them he again saw many remarkable feats of magic. But he was never able to discover how these illusions were created.

T I B E T

Since the Khan did not desire Marco to penetrate deeply into the land of Tibet, he did not go to the sacred city of Lhasa. This sacred city, which is perhaps the most inaccessible city in the entire world, has even to this day rarely been visited by travellers.

Instead of proceeding deeper into Tibet, Marco Polo, having accomplished in this part of Cathay what the Khan required, turned southward to visit the provinces on the borderland of India. These lands were known as Assam and Burma. And Marco found them strange lands with strange customs.

CHAPTER XVII

CROCODILES AND EVIL SPIRITS

On his way through the southern provinces of Cathay, Marco Polo came to a place where the natives hunted crocodiles. Never having seen one before, he called them "great serpents".

He made note of the fact that some of these "great serpents" were terribly large and hideously ugly, with enormous heads garnished with great pointed teeth.

The natives of this land captured these monsters in this way. At night when the crocodiles came out of their cool caverns in search of food and drink, they dragged themselves toward some lake or river. Because of their great weight and clumsy movements they made paths through the woods. When the natives found one of these tracks, made by a large crocodile, they got some small blades of steel which had been sharpened to a keen razor's edge. These blades they buried in the path with the sharp edges projecting above the surface of the ground. They covered the blades over with loose sand and dried leaves. Then, when the great crocodile crawled along the path and dragged his heavy weight over the sharp knives, the soft underpart of his body was ripped open. As soon as he was mortally wounded, the crows began to caw and fly overhead. This told the natives exactly where they could find the monster who, now weak from his wounds, was unable to resist capture. The fresh meat of crocodiles was considered a great delicacy. And the natives also carefully remove the gall from the body of this reptile, making it into medicine.

This medicine was considered most effective against the bite of a mad dog, for the labour pains of women in childbirth and the skin eruptions on the body.

It was also on this southern journey that Marco Polo encountered a race of people who practiced a very strange custom. When a woman in this part of the country gave birth to a child, as soon as the child was washed and swathed she rose from her bed and returned to her household duties. And the moment she got out of bed, her husband climbed into the bed and remained there with the newborn baby. These people thought that the husband should have a share in the birth of his child and should help in the "hatching".

And so the man—in bed with the baby—was visited by all his neighbours, who were always in a very festive mood on such occasions. In the meantime, the mother had the job of caring for both her husband and her baby while they were lying in bed. This kept up for many days. At length, when the father thought that the baby was well "hatched" and that no more brooding was necessary, he would get out of bed and go back to work.

Marco Polo recorded this strange custom as a great curiosity, and he was sure that few people would believe it to be a fact. He did not, however, know that the same custom was practised at that time in many other parts of the world. Neither could he know that in such places as Spain and South America, this custom would continue into modern times. This primitive practice is called "couvade".

Marco also found that the people in some of these southern lands did not worship idols and had no temples. Instead, they worshipped their forefathers. "We worship him from whom we have sprung," they said simply.

And when one of these same people was taken ill, the relatives sent for their magicians who were devil conjurers. These conjurers, arriving at the home of the sick man, first talked with him to find out where his pains were located. Then they played on instruments and began singing and dancing. As their singing grew louder, their dancing became wilder until it reached a pitch of frenzy. This they kept up until one of their number fell to the ground in a faint. When this happened, they truly believed that the devil had entered the body of the swooned magician. As he recovered consciousness his comrades crowded about him and asked him questions about the sick man's ailment. Then he would reply: "A certain evil spirit has been meddling with this man because he has been angered!" The magician would then call out the name of the offended spirit and all would kneel and pray, begging the evil spirit to forgive the sick man and restore him to health.

Sometimes these devil conjurers claimed that they could speak directly with the evil spirit. And often they reported that the spirit had ordered a feast to be held in his honour, otherwise he would not allow the sick man to recover! In this event the family at once prepared the feast, demanded by the spirit, and invited a suitable number of ladies and family friends.

Everyone drank wine and ate the good things which had been prepared. Everyone sang and danced until they could sing and dance no more. Then one of the devil conjurers would fall to the ground and cry out to the spirit: "Has he been pardoned yet?" If the answer was "no" then the feast and dancing continued. But if the answer was "yes", then it was announced with joy that the spirit had pardoned the sick man, and that he would soon recover.

When this happy announcement was made, all would once more fall to eating and drinking. Before, they ate and drank in honour of the spirit, but now they feasted because of happiness. At length, when everyone was exhausted, the devil conjurers and the invited guests departed for their homes.

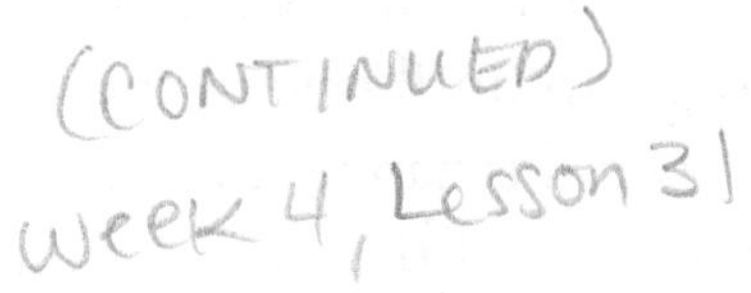

CHAPTER XVIII

BURMESE GOLD

CROSSING OVER A long range of mountains, Marco Polo continued his journey into the southern province of Burma. For several days he followed a downhill road until he came to open plains.

Here he found a small town centred around an open market where all kinds of produce was exchanged. Three days a week the natives came down from the hills, bringing with them gold which they exchanged for silver. Merchants from distant provinces came here to buy this gold, for the natives sold it at the cheap rate of one piece of gold for five of silver. Elsewhere, one was required to pay ten or even fifteen pieces of silver for one piece of gold.

The natives found the gold nuggets in the hills not far from this market. But they would not disclose the exact place. Neither would they suffer anyone to follow them into this region.

At length, after travelling fifteen days from this market place, Marco arrived at the city of Mien, the capital of the province of Burma. The country through which he now travelled was completely uninhabited, and the dense forests abounded with herds of wild elephants, rhinoceroses, leopards and tigers.

The city of Mien was large and rich. And among the many splendours which Marco found there were two towers, one of gold and one of silver. These towers flanked the tomb of a dead king. They were not in truth made of solid gold and silver, but rather of stone upon which the pure metals had been applied—almost an inch in thickness.

THE CITY OF MIEN

Marco noted that these rare towers were about thirty feet high. And the spire of each tower was circled by a ring of bells which sounded their pleasant chimes as they swayed gently in the breeze.

These beautiful towers of gold and silver caught the rays of the bright sun; they sparkled brilliantly and were seen by travellers from a great distance away.

Some years before, when the Khan's soldiers conquered Burma, they considered peeling the heavy gold and silver from the towers and sending it to Cambalu as loot. But when the Khan was informed of this intention, he replied by fast messenger that these towers must not be violated because they had been erected in memory of a departed king.

The Mongols, Marco Polo observed, were most superstitious and would not touch anything which they thought might belong to the spirit of someone who was dead.

Farther south and east, crossing the border of Burma, Marco Polo came into the province of Kangigu. This province was governed by a king who was very rich and devoted to pleasure. Whenever he heard of a truly beautiful woman in his domain, he sent for her and married her. In this manner he had acquired three hundred wives!

In this land rich spices were grown and large quantities of gold were found. And tamed elephants were used to carry all heavy burdens.

Marco also noted that here both the men and women had their bodies heavily tattooed in elaborate designs of animals, birds, dragons and flowers. This work was done by special artists who were highly skilled and whose workmanship was so delicate that it resembled fine embroidery.

Close by, in another province, Marco found that the men and women wore great numbers of gold bracelets on their arms and legs. They raised horses, buffaloes and oxen which they sold to India. He remarked that he saw no poor people in this province, for all seemed to enjoy the rich abundance of their land.

In still another province, not far from Burma, Marco Polo found a people who made a cloth from the bark of certain trees. The bark was first boiled and then beaten into a soft pulp, after which it was worked into a material called grass cloth. This material was very light and delightfully cool to wear.

In this land, tigers were so numerous that the inhabitants lived in constant fear. "We dare not venture out of town at night," they said. "And those who navigate the river cannot rest with their boats moored near the banks. Tigers have been known to plunge into the water, swim to a boat and attacked the man." To protect themselves against these tigers the natives bred very large fierce dogs. These dogs were bold enough to give chase and hold the tiger at bay until hunters could arrive and kill the beast.

Throughout all these five provinces of the South, Marco Polo travelled as a special envoy of the Khan. After he had visited these territories and performed all those things which he had to do for the Khan, he started back to Cathay.

He now journeyed north along the China Sea and entered Cathay at its most southerly boundary.

THE RIVER KARAMORAN

CHAPTER XIX

HANCHOW, CITY OF HEAVEN

ARCO FOUND THE southern provinces of Cathay to be rich, fertile and densely populated. Many rivers and streams watered the green farm lands.

Here, in the most southerly part of Cathay, he saw the terminal of a great canal that ran northward overland, crossing many rivers and cutting through many hills until it reached the capital city of Cambalu.

This Grand Canal, which in Chinese is called "the river of locks" or "transport river", was begun long before the Mongols conquered Cathay. With the coming of Genghis, work on the canal was abandoned, but when Kublai Khan came to the throne he at once recognized the importance of this waterway to the commerce of his country. He therefore ordered that the work be resumed and the canal extended to connect Cambalu with the great city of Canton in southern China. Thousands of prisoners and slaves were sent to work on the project. This great waterway, built to aid commerce through easy transportation of produce and merchandise, remains to this very day one of the outstanding engineering feats of the world. On the banks of the many rivers that flow through this fertile land, Marco found rich and beautiful cities. Here trade flourished. Many ships sailed the rivers laden with merchandise and farm products. The merchants gained great profits from manufacture and trade. They lived in fine houses surrounded by orchards and gardens.

And each of these great cities on the banks of the rivers in southern

Cathay paid taxes to the Khan. His revenue was so great from this section of his land that he took special care to see that the people were content with his rule. He knew that discontented people often refused to pay their taxes.

In each city Marco Polo saw the governor and in the name of the Khan inquired about the wellbeing of the people. He made note of all matters that they desired brought to the Khan's attention.

Thus, in pursuit of his duties, Marco travelled northward until he reached the city of Hanchow[1]. This city, Marco thought, was one of the finest cities in the entire world and was truly, as its name implies, the City of Heaven.

Hanchow reminded him of his native Venice. It was situated between a beautiful lake and a river which supplied the water for hundreds of canals that laced through the city. It also had many wide streets and one was able to travel through it either by boat or by carriage.

The thousands of beautiful stone bridges, highly arched across its many canals, gave this city a special grandeur. It was said that there were twelve thousand bridges in Hanchow and these were so skilfully built—with arches so high—that vessels with masts could pass under them. At the same time, the ramps were so sloped that horses and carts could pass over them.

There were within the city ten large market places and also innumerable streets with shops. Here was sold merchandise from all parts of the kingdom, as well as from distant lands such as India.

Marco found these markets filled with good food that was sold at a cheap price. He made note of the various kinds of game and fowl that one could buy. There were, among other things, roebuck, red deer, fallow deer, hares, rabbits, partridges, pheasants, quails, fowls, capons and many kinds of geese and ducks. For a single silver coin, one could buy two geese and four ducks.

These market places also supplied the people with fresh beef and lamb, as well as a great variety of fish brought, fresh each day, twenty-

1 Also called Kinsai.

THE CITY OF KINSAI

five miles up the river from the sea. Vegetables and fruit were in great abundance. And Marco noted that they were the finest grown anywhere. The pears, he said, were most fragrant and the peaches, both yellow and white, had a very delicate flavour.

Here in this beautiful city Marco Polo found twelve guilds of craftsmen. Each guild had many workshops which made things of rare beauty. Because these wares were in great demand, the workmen—and the master craftsmen over them—were constantly occupied from one end of the year to the other. The things they made, with much art and skill, were sold all over Cathay.

The merchants of this city enjoyed great prosperity and lived in princely splendour. Their wives were most beautiful and enjoyed many luxuries. They dressed in silks and finely woven brocades.

At night special sentries patrolled the city streets to enforce the curfew and protect the city. Absolutely no one was allowed on the streets at night after a certain time. At each hour these sentries struck a gong to mark the passing of time. They also watched the streets and homes to see that there were no disturbances, and they kept a sharp look-out for fires. Should a fire occur, the sentries gave the alarm by beating on gongs with great mallets.

At the sound of this fire alarm the watchmen from all the bridges within a certain distance came to help extinguish the flames. Even at such times, the people were not permitted to break the curfew by leaving their homes. Only the people whose home was on fire were allowed to join the fire fighters. What could be saved from the flames was carried away and placed in stone towers for safe keeping. These towers were maintained by the city for such emergencies.

On the large lake which bordered one side of the city there were many pleasure boats. And after the day's work was done the people delighted in taking their families and friends for a ride across the water. Along the shores of this lake could be seen palaces, temples and gardens which sloped down to the water's edge. Hanchow also had many beautiful parks and bathing pools, some of them large enough to accommodate one hundred people at a time. The people of this city seemed to take much pleasure from the great variety and beauty of nature.

All in all, Marco Polo was highly impressed with the cultured life in Hanchow. The people, he found, were well dressed, well mannered and enjoyed good food and good living. They lived in peace and avoided feuds and quarrels. They were completely honest and displayed good will toward each other.

It was the duty of Marco Polo to speak with the Khan's tax collectors as well as with the city officials. From this city the tax on salt alone brought the Khan a great fortune each year. And a ten per cent tax on sugar, silk and other merchandise, domestic and imported, also went to the Khan. In short, when all the revenues were added together, the Khan received each year from this rich city a fortune that was counted in millions. So it was no wonder that the Great Khan considered it a most favoured place and that he watched carefully to see that the administration was well conducted and that the people were content with his rule. For Hanchow was truly the City of Heaven.

To the north of Hanchow, Marco Polo came to another large and magnificent city called Soochow. It was also a city of great wealth, for here the people had vast quantities of raw silk which they manufactured into beautiful material. This silk was sold all over Cathay. Soochow was at that time, as it is to-day, one of the great silk centres of Cathay.

Just north of Soochow, Marco Polo came to the Yangtse River. "This river," he said, "must surely be the greatest river in all the world. In some places it is ten miles wide and its length is such that it takes one hundred days to travel from its source to its mouth."

He also said that this great river passed through sixteen provinces and had along its shores two hundred cities and countless towns and villages. In one large city along its banks he saw moored fifteen thousand vessels at one time. And he estimated that within a single year 200,000 vessels sailed the river. These figures were confirmed by the Khan's revenue collectors whose duty it was to collect taxes from each ship that carried merchandise on the Yangtse.

The ships that sailed this river were constructed to carry great quantities of merchandise of all kinds. The principal commodity, however, was salt. Salt was brought from the coast upstream, far into the interior of Cathay.

It was near the banks of the Yangtse that Marco Polo visited the city of Sa-Yan-Fu. He was particularly interested in visiting this city because many years before his father Nicolo and his uncle Maffeo had contributed to its capture by the armies of the great Khan.

It happened that the Khan's troops besieged Sa-Yan-Fu for three long years and still it refused to surrender. This grieved the Khan. And when Nicolo and Maffeo—who were then staying at the court—heard of this they offered a solution. They proposed to the Khan that with the help of carpenters and blacksmiths they should build for his army certain military machines like those used in Europe. These machines, capable of hurling three-hundred-pound rocks upon the enemy, were unknown in the Orient.

When after a few days these machines were completed, a trial test was made for the Khan and his whole court. Everyone was much impressed with these rock hurlers. And so they were quickly sent to the besieging army.

The machines were set up before the walled city of Sa-Yan-Fu. The very first rock projected fell with such force upon a building that it crushed it to the ground. Seeing this, the inhabitants of the city were filled with terror, for they believed that the rock had fallen from heaven. They immediately surrendered!

Travelling farther north, Marco Polo came again to the great Yellow River. This time he crossed the river close to its mouth. At this point it is a mile wide and very deep. And like the Yangtse it, too, was used as a great waterway.

At one place on this river, about a mile up from the sea, Marco

Polo visited a great fleet of fifteen thousand warships belonging to the Khan. Each ship was capable of carrying fifteen horses and twenty men, beside the crew to navigate it and necessary stores and provisions. The Khan kept this fleet, ever ready, to convey an army to any of his dominions near India that might happen to revolt.

After crossing the Yellow River Marco Polo found himself once more close to Cambalu and the court of Kublai Khan. He journeyed on and in a few days more was back home in the palace. He was weary but happy to be back with the Khan and to see his father and uncle again. And the Khan, too, was happy to have him safely returned to his court.

CHAPTER XX

FOOD FOR THE HUNGRY

DURING THE DAYS that followed Marco Polo's return to the court, he spent many long hours with the Khan.

He gave the Khan a full account of his long trip: of the lands through which he had passed, the people, the industries, agriculture and the natural wealth. The Khan was greatly interested for he felt that all this information was invaluable to him as ruler of this vast domain. And in recognition of Marco's service to Cathay, the Khan presented him with many gifts and robes of honour.

Now it happened, when Marco returned to the court, that his father Nicolo and his uncle Maffeo came to him.

"We have now been in Cathay for many years," they said. "And although life here is very pleasant, still we long to return home to Venice."

Marco was not completely in agreement with their wish. "I am very happy here in Cathay," he said. "It is a wonderful land of wonderful people. To me it is ever exciting and interesting. Besides, here at the court I hold an important position. If I return to Venice I will be only a merchant."

However, since the elder Polos were eager to return to Venice, Marco consented to speak to the Khan on this matter.

But when Marco suggested to the Khan that he and his father and uncle might return to Venice, the Khan was greatly disturbed and tried in every way to hold them. To lose these friends would he a great sorrow to him, the very thought of which he could not bear.

And so he said that he would never let them go and he did not want Marco ever to bring up this subject again. He now doubled his efforts to make the Polos happy and content in his palace. And soon the Polos forgot about their native Venice and settled down again to a busy life in Cambalu.

During the years that followed, Marco served the Khan Kublai faithfully and well. From time to time he went on special missions. When a matter seemed urgent and required an unbiased report, it was Marco who was chosen to undertake the task.

One year the Khan sent Marco to a distant province that had suffered a great drought and was appealing for relief. He wanted Marco to act as his commissioner and supervise the distribution of the grain and cattle that he was sending to this district.

It was the policy of the Khan to fill his state granaries in times of plenty so that in times of necessity there would be sufficient for relief. Any person or community in need could apply directly to the Khan for help. The Khan would supply not only sufficient grain for food, but also enough for planting the following spring. He also replaced all cattle that had perished through disaster. Through his great network of roads and waterways, he sent relief quickly to any section of Cathay that might be suffering from droughts, storms, locusts or other pests.

But besides buying grain to fill his granaries in years of plenty, to support the people of his land in times of hunger, the Khan also took pity on the poor. He saw to it that they did not starve and that they were given clothing.

Poor families in many cities received wheat and other grains sufficient for food for a whole year. And this was repeated as long as the relief was necessary. Many times in many places Marco saw long lines of poor receiving bowls of rice and grains daily.

Clothing, too, was provided for the needy. All weavers, dyers and tailors were required to work one day of each week in the Khan's shops producing materials and clothing for the poor.

AN AGRICULTURAL COMMISSIONE

All this the Khan did out of pity for those in need. His Mongol forefathers did not feel such pity. They did not believe in helping the poor; in fact, they were hard and cruel and drove beggars away with such words as: "Go with God's curse, for if He loved you, as He loves me, He would have provided for you."

And by reason of this admirable and astonishing generosity toward the unfortunate and the poor, the people of Cathay adored the Khan.

After Marco had returned from the drought-stricken area where he had supervised the distribution of relief, the Khan needed his services again on another matter. The Khan having learnt of great corruption among his officials in Yang-Chau, and having ordered them all to be arrested, appointed Marco governor of this city. It was Marco's task as governor to reorganize the many different departments of the city of Yang-Chau. It was his duty to see that they once more functioned properly and honestly. This task took three long years.

When Marco again returned to Cambalu he found the Khan in a despondent mood. "My great royal armada," said the Khan, "which I sent out to conquer the islands of Japan, has been completely destroyed! Every vessel—with its full company of sailors and soldiers—has been lost! This is not the first armada which I have sent against Japan. And this is not the first to have been destroyed. All have been destroyed! Some have been destroyed by storms at sea, some have been dashed against Japan's rocky coast and some have been sunk by the unconquerable Japanese."

The vessels which the Khan built to send against Japan were constructed of heavy fir planks. They were patterned after the traditional junks of Cathay. Each vessel carried four masts and had a great rudder at the stern, which was so constructed that it could be raised in shallow water. The heavy planks were nailed together with iron spikes and the entire outer surface made waterproof. This waterproofing compound, Marco Polo noted, was made of lime, hemp fibres and a special oil extracted from trees. The mixture was painted over the planks of the junk and made them completely waterproof.

While the many war junks were being built for the Khan on the shores of Cathay, he gathered his armies in the land of Korea. For Korea, which belonged to the Khan, was close to the islands of Japan. And when his vessels were ready, they came to Korea and here the soldiers embarked. Many sailed but few returned.

The Mongols, who were famous horsemen, understood how to conquer by land, but they did not understand the ways of the sea. No armada that the Khan ever sent against Japan was able to conquer these islands.

While Marco Polo never saw Japan, he met people who had been there and he heard many stories of this land. He recorded what he heard about these islands which we now know were not visited by Europeans until several hundred years after his time. He learnt that the entire roof of the emperor's palace was covered with fine gold and that the ceilings of the royal halls were covered in the same manner. He was also told that in many of the royal apartments there were small tables of pure gold, and that in the waters surrounding these islands were found large pink pearls in great quantities. Marco said that these pink pearls greatly exceeded white pearls in value.

There was still another part of Asia which Marco was unable to visit but in which he was very interested. These were the northern lands of Mongolia, Siberia and the Arctic Region. In the days of Marco Polo the vast territory of Siberia, which contains more than five million square miles, did not belong to Russia but was ruled over by Mongolian chieftains and chieftains of other tribes.

Marco Polo often spoke with envoys that came to the Khan from these northern territories. He learned that the most important chieftain of these northern lands was a Mongol and a cousin of the great Khan. He learned, too, that these northern people had no cities and that their chieftains had no palaces. They wandered about from place to place with great herds of grazing cattle—they were master breeders of cattle, horses, camels, oxen, sheep and other domestic animals.

Marco was told of the rich wild life of these northern plains. Here

THE LAND OF DARKNESS

were found pure white bears of great size, large black foxes and great abundance of sables and ermines.

The natives sent these costly pelts to markets in far-off countries, receiving in exchange many kinds of goods which in their lands they were unable to grow or produce.

Marco also learnt of a curious thing that was then unknown in Europe; the tribes of the Far North, where there was much snow, rode in sledges drawn by dogs! And still farther north, it seemed that there were lands of darkness. During the long winters the sun refused to shine and a perpetual twilight was over the entire country. Here in these snowy regions the people were quite savage; they had no rulers and they lived by hunting and fishing.

All these facts Marco wrote down among his notes while he was at the Khan's court in Cambalu.

CHAPTER XXI

AMBASSADORS FROM PERSIA

NOW IT HAPPENED that after the Polos had been in Cambalu for eighteen years, there arrived at the court of the great Khan three ambassadors from Persia. These ambassadors had undertaken this long journey for a very special reason. The beautiful queen, Bolgana of Persia, had died and they had come to inform the Khan of this sad news. The Khan was greatly concerned because the beautiful queen had, many years before, been a lady of his court. She had been a lady of great culture and beauty and the Khan had presented her to the king of Persia in a gesture of friendship. The king had immediately fallen in love with her and had made her his queen. Now she was dead.

The ambassadors from the king of Persia had journeyed the long distance with a request.

"Our gracious king," they said, "is so deeply grieved at the loss of his beautiful queen that he begs you, O noble Khan, to present him with another bride. He desires one equal in culture and beauty, one from the same family as his favoured queen Bolgana."

The three ambassadors then promised that if the Khan would grant this favour, they would escort the bride safely back to Persia.

The Khan was pleased to concede to this request. He was glad to have someone from his own court on the throne of Persia. He felt that this would strengthen the ties between his court and Cambalu and this far-distant dominion of his empire. Therefore, the Khan immediately consulted with the special commissioners, those who each year chose the one hundred new beauties for the court, and soon he made his choice.

He selected a certain princess whose name was Lady Cocachin[2]. She was of the same family as the late queen and in many ways resembled her. Lady Cocachin, while only a maiden of seventeen, had great charm and great beauty.

The Khan sent for her and spoke with her privately. He asked her if she would be willing to marry the king of Persia and if she would be willing to undertake so long a journey. He told her that he would provide her with a dowry that would be worthy of a queen. He also told her that Argon, the king of Persia, was quite handsome and a gentle person. And if she consented to this marriage she would then share the throne of a great and rich land.

Lady Cocachin nodded. She was willing.

When she was presented to the three Persian ambassadors they found her most charming and beautiful. They could see at a glance that she resembled their late queen and they lost no time in declaring that the lady pleased them well. She was everything that they could possibly have hoped for.

A happy excitement now filled the palace. Lady Cocachin was being prepared for her long journey. Her trousseau, more magnificent than any that had ever before been seen in Cathay, was being assembled. The ladies of the court helped select and order the gowns and other things that she would take with her to Persia. And the Khan showered her with rare gems and costly jewelry. He took a personal interest in every detail.

Now, when Nicolo and Maffeo Polo heard that Lady Cocachin was to be sent to Persia, they were once more filled with a longing to return to their homeland. They spoke about this to Marco. They explained to him that they were no longer young and that they feared that if they waited longer they would be too old to undertake such an arduous journey. In that case, they would never see Venice again.

2 Sometimes referred to as Kogatin.

RINCESS KOGATIN

"The great Khan," said Nicolo, "is now seventy-six years old, and if he should die, the new ruler may not be so well disposed toward strangers in the court."

"Yes," agreed Maffeo. "A new ruler might not be friendly to us. I think it would therefore be wise for us to join Lady Cocachin and the ambassadors. We could travel with them as far as Persia. Then from Persia we could travel on alone to Europe."

Marco was not eager to leave Cathay but he could see the wisdom of this plan. Accordingly, the three Polos went to see the great Khan. But when the Khan heard of their plan he was still reluctant to give his consent. He reminded them that many years before he had asked them never again to bring up this subject. And he asked them now to put all such thoughts out of their minds.

In due time, when everything was ready, Lady Cocachin and the three ambassadors left the court of Kublai Khan. The long procession, carrying hundreds of boxes filled with her trousseau, was headed by the three Persians on horseback and protected by a heavy detachment of soldiers from the Khan's garrison.

But Marco Polo, his father Nicolo and his uncle Maffeo remained behind in Cambalu.

CHAPTER XXII

"WHEN WE SAY GOOD-BYE IT WILL BE FOREVER"

FEW MONTHS LATER, news of Lady Cocachin and the three ambassadors came to the palace by the Khan's fast post-riders.

The procession had been stopped on the borderland of one of the western countries. Here they were forced to await the outcome of a long series of battles. Even with the Khan's armed guard it was not possible for them to force through with safety. And, since they carried with them a bride and a small treasure in the form of a trousseau, they could not risk this passage.

Later more dispatches arrived. Finally the Khan was informed that the ambassadors considered it useless to wait, and therefore the entire party was returning to Cambalu without delay.

The Khan was worried. What could he do? How could he deliver this bride from Cathay to the king of Persia?

Now Marco Polo came forward with a plan.

"There is a way," he said to the Khan, "and only one way to avoid the long overland journey. There is a water route. As you well know, merchants from Cathay frequently navigate the southern waters to India. And after rounding India it is possible to sail on through the Arabian Sea then through the straits that divide Arabia from Persia. Once through these straits, one is in the Gulf of Persia. Then from the coast of this gulf to the capital of Persia is but a short overland journey. Lady Cocachin's party would, of course, on this overland trip, have the protection of the king of Persia.

To this the Khan replied that he desired to see the charts. How was it possible to sail around India?

When the charts were unrolled before him, Marco Polo traced the journey which would take Lady Cocachin's party along the coast of southern Cathay to the lands of Malay and Sumatra, then to Ceylon, India and on to Persia. Many times he assured the Khan that if the vessels were properly constructed then the journey could be made with ease and safety. And while it was a long voyage, dependent upon wind and tide, still it would take no longer than the hard journey overland.

The Khan listened carefully to Marco's recommendations. Then he studied the charts in silence for a long time. Finally he turned to Marco and spoke slowly.

"As you can see I am now an old man, seventy-six years of age. And I know that it will not be many more years before I join my honourable ancestors. I have been thinking of this in recent times and I have also thought of you and your father and uncle. And although I am greatly attached to all of you and our parting will be very difficult, I feel that I have no right to hold you any longer. We have all been good friends and we have been very fortunate to have had so many happy years together. But now we must part. You have all served me faithfully through the years and you will serve me once more by escorting Lady Cocachin to Persia."

The Khan now asked that Nicolo and Maffeo Polo should be summoned. When they appeared he informed them of his decision.

All three Polos bowed low before the Khan and thanked him for his great kindness. They promised that they would guard the bride from Cathay with their lives, and that they would deliver her safely to Argon, the king of Persia. They also told the Khan that the many years that they had spent in his court would ever remain with them as a happy memory. And they vowed that he would always be with them in their hearts.

Now the Khan and the Polos discussed the plans for the long voyage. The Khan was interested in knowing how many ships and mariners

HE BATTLE BETWEEN ARGON AND ACOMAT

would be necessary. He also wanted to know about the provisions and all the other details.

"As you already know," said Marco, "my father and uncle have had much experience with vessels. In fact they own a number of merchant ships that ply between the ports of Europe and Constantinople. They know how a vessel should be designed to outride a storm. And they know how large the crews should be and what provisions are necessary." The Khan nodded. Yes, all this he already knew. And so he entrusted Nicolo and Maffeo with all the arrangements for the flotilla.

Remodelling of the necessary ships was begun at once. And all the other preparations for the voyage were so well attended to that everything was ready by the time Lady Cocachin and the three ambassadors returned to Cambalu. Eight months had passed since Lady Cocachin had first left the court. But now she had returned and was pleased to learn that her journey to Persia had not been abandoned.

Now, while the flotilla was being made ready, the Polos were also very busy with their own affairs. For since they were leaving Cathay forever, it was necessary for them to dispose of their warehouse and all their merchandise. They also had to sell many personal things that they had acquired during their long years of residence in Cathay. With the money they bought jewels and small precious objects which were easy to carry. They bought rubies, emeralds, pearls and diamonds. And all these precious gems they carefully concealed by sewing them in the linings of their woollen garments. In this way they secured hundreds and hundreds of valuable gems.

They had boxes made to hold some of the costly presents given to them by the Khan. And being merchants, and knowing well what Europe lacked and what was cheap in the Orient, they bought quantities of such things as silks, musk and rare spices. If they could manage to bring these things back with them to Europe, they knew that a small fortune would result from their sale.

Every day they worked hard at the task of getting ready to depart. In this they were aided by the three ambassadors.

At length the day arrived.

The Khan had grown to love Marco, and Marco had acquired a deep respect for this ruler. Their parting was not easy.

"I cannot ask you to return again to Cathay," said the Khan. "I am now old and so when we say good-bye it will be forever and forever. There is no need to tell you how much your visit has meant to me. For your friendship, your loyalty, your courage and your long devoted service, there is no adequate reward. You have served me for eighteen years. It is now twenty-one years since you left your home. May the gods bring you back to your native land safely. And may you live long and think kindly of me always."

When the Khan had spoken these words he drew the ring off his finger and put it on Marco Polo's finger. This was his last present to the young man he had grown to love.

CHAPTER XXIII

THE VOYAGE HOME

THE KHAN APPOINTED the Polos as commanders of the entire bridal flotilla, which consisted of thirteen vessels. He gave them complete authority, and hung from the neck of each his golden tablet so that at any port within his dominions they might command what they required.

He also gave them friendly letters to the kings of England, France and Spain.

He assured Lady Cocachin and the three ambassadors that the Polos were master navigators and that under their command her party would reach the far-off port in Persia without difficulty.

All this the Khan spoke from the throne in the great hall of the palace where a vast crowd had gathered to witness this final farewell.

At length, when the Khan was finished speaking all who were about to depart—the Polos, Lady Cocachin, the ambassadors and their personal aides—all bowed low. They touched their foreheads four times to the floor to show their deep respect for the Khan. Then they left his presence.

Lady Cocachin was carried to the coast in a royal palanquin, while the Polos and the three Persian ambassadors rode on white horses. They were accompanied by a guard of honour of the Khan's soldiers.

At the coast they found the vessels ready to depart. As soon as all had embarked, the sails were hoisted and the vessels set out to sea.

Marco Polo watched the coast line, as it receded into the distance, until he could see it no longer. This was his last glimpse of wonderful Cathay.

J A V A

During the next eighteen months the Polos and their flotilla sailed through many bodies of water. They sailed through the Yellow Sea, the Eastern Sea, through the straits that separate the island of Formosa from the mainland, through the China Sea, across the Bay of Bengal, over part of the Indian Ocean, through the Arabian Sea and finally into the Persian Gulf.

This was a year and a half of great sea adventure. They touched many ports—many lands—and saw many strange races.

After calling at several ports in Indo-China and in the Malay Peninsula, Marco Polo visited the island of Java. He recorded that he found this island wealthy and filled with treasures. Here were grown white pepper as well as black pepper, nutmegs, spikenard, cloves and many other valuable spices and herbs. Merchants brought their ships into the ports of Java and sailed away laden with the rich produce from which they gained great profits.

The next large island that they visited was Sumatra. Here Marco found eight kingdoms governed by as many kings. Each nation had a language of its own and the people of Sumatra, for the most part, were Mohammedans.

There were, however, certain natives who lived in the mountains in a most primitive way practicing cannibalism. Marco also noted that in Sumatra there were wild elephants, rhinoceroses, monkeys of all kinds and huge black vultures.

They now sailed on to the Nicobar Islands, where they took on fresh water and supplies. Then crossing the Bay of Bengal, the flotilla came to the island of Ceylon off the coast of India. Here, on this island, there were many wonderful things for Marco Polo to see.

In Ceylon were found beautiful rubies, sapphires, topazes, amethysts and garnets. The king of this land was reported to have the largest ruby in the world. It was said to be without a single flaw and to have the appearance of a glowing fire. The great Khan had once tried to buy this ruby, but the king had answered that he would not sell it for all the treasure of the universe. Nor would he ever allow

THE ISLAND OF CEYLON

it to leave his land, for it had been handed down to him, through generations, by all the former kings of Ceylon.

It was also on this island that Marco saw a very high rocky mountain. On the top of this mountain was a tomb said to be that of Adam, the first man. One could visit the tomb and also see some holy relics—teeth, a few wisps of hair and a beautiful vessel of green stone, all of which were reported to have belonged to Adam. Visitors reached the high summit by means of iron chains, which had been installed for this purpose. But there were some in Ceylon who did not believe this. They claimed that it was Buddha, not Adam, who was buried on this mountain top.

Marco also noted that the people of Ceylon, because of the great heat, wore only a light cloth wrapped around the middle of their bodies.

Leaving the island of Ceylon and sailing westward only a short distance, the flotilla reached India. It sailed up the coast and stopped at many ports of this great land. At every port Marco spoke with the people and gathered all the information he could about their country.

This country, Marco found, was made up of numerous kingdoms. Those of the South had a very hot climate, while those of the North, where there were mountains, enjoyed a cooler climate. The people for the most part were Mohammedans and Buddhists. And because of their religion, many people of this land would not kill any animal, wild or domestic, not even a bird, insect or reptile. They ate only grain, milk, fruit and vegetables.

Now Marco heard that in a certain part of this great country there were streams in which diamonds were found. These diamonds were usually gathered after the rainy season. The rain water, rushing down the mountain streams in great torrents, washed away quantities of sand and gravel and exposed the beds of diamonds. These diamonds were then collected after the rains had ceased and the rushing streams had dried up.

At one place along the coast of India Marco saw men diving for

HE PEARLS OF MAABAR

pearls. They held their breath and were able to remain under water for a long time. When they rose to the surface their net bags were filled with pearl-bearing oysters. These pearls were very large and round and of fine lustre.

Marco Polo noted that one of the strangest customs in all the world was practiced here in India. When a man died, his relatives, with great rejoicing, formed a funeral procession and carried his body to the place of cremation. Now the dead man's wife, to show her great regard for her departed husband, threw herself on the pyre and was also consumed by the flames. Any widow who shrank from this act was despised and insulted in her community. This custom was called "suttee" and continued for many centuries after Marco's visit.

Here in India, too, there were many experts in the prediction of future events. These people could foretell the future through beasts and birds. They especially studied the flight of birds, from which they predicted good or evil fortune. There were also many people in this country who regarded one particular hour of each week as unlucky; and during this hour they would not make any purchases or transact any business.

These are only a very few of the many things which Marco heard and saw in the great land of India.

There was one thing more, however, which he heard.

He was told of a great island, approximately fifteen hundred miles south-west of India in the Indian Ocean. This island was called Madagascar. The natives of this island claimed that at a certain season of the year an extraordinarily large bird, which they called a "roe", flew over the island. It came from the southern regions and they claimed that it resembled an eagle but was much greater in size. In fact it was so large that it could lift a baby elephant into the air and drop it again on the ground in order to kill it, after which it would feast on the carcass.

According to *The Arabian Nights,* this was the same bird that lifted Sinbad the sailor and transported him to distant lands. Marco

R U K H

Polo doubted that such a huge bird could exist, but still he recorded faithfully what he was told. And this was one of the stories, which later his friends in Venice found hard to believe. Yet, in recent years, the shell of a huge egg was found in these regions. This shell is now in a British museum. Its capacity is about two and one-third gallons!

Now the flotilla bearing Lady Cocachin and the three ambassadors sailed on toward the Persian Gulf. After several more months of voyaging the party finally reached the coast of Persia. Here they were happy to disembark.

From the coast of Persia, Lady Cocachin, the ambassadors, and the Polos, together with a guard of men, journeyed inland until they came to the palace of the king. They had come from Cathay—a long journey—safely to their final destination.

But now, alas, they heard bad news. The good king Argon, who was to receive Lady Cocachin as his bride, had died and his son Casan was now the ruler of Persia.

However, the new king admired the beautiful Lady Cocachin and ordered that, since his good father was dead, she should be delivered to him. At this the Polos were quite disturbed for Casan was not as handsome as his father; in fact he was quite ugly. And the Polos feared that Lady Cocachin might not desire him. But their fears were groundless for she was quite willing to become his wife—and queen of Persia.

With this mission safely executed, the Polos were now free to depart for their native home in Venice. But before they left Persia they were greatly honoured by the young king and the three ambassadors. And they came away with many very beautiful presents.

Their journey overland now took them through northern Persia and Turkey to the shore of the Black Sea. Many servants and pack horses helped them carry the goods which they were bringing with them. On the coast of the Black Sea they charted a vessel and sailed for Constantinople, then into the Mediterranean and finally up the coast of Italy to their native city of Venice.

At last, at last, after an absence of twenty-four years they were back in the city of their birth.

Many of the streets seemed changed. Many new buildings had been erected. But they knew their way to the old Polo house, their old home.

CHAPTER XXIV

THE ROAD TO CATHAY IS CLOSED

STRAY DOGS, BARKING at their heels, followed the Polos through the streets of Venice.

Their clothes were old and torn. It was now three years since they had left the court of Kublai Khan. The bundles that they carried were tied in oriental cloths. Their hats and shoes seemed very queer. In fact everything about them bore the strange stamp of the Tartar.

When the Polos reached their old home the dogs did not stop barking. They followed them through the gateway and into the courtyard. Here the three travellers put down their bundles and knocked at the door.

But the servant who answered was frightened. Believing that these three were beggars or vagabonds, he shouted at them and ordered them to leave at once. It was not until some relatives had been sent for that they were recognized and allowed to enter their old home, which was now inhabited by cousins and other members of the large Polo family.

The news soon spread throughout Venice that the Polo brothers and young Marco had returned. It was exciting news. For many years these three had been given up for dead. But now they were back. Where had they been all this time?

"It must have been far away," said some, "otherwise they could have sent a message of some kind to their old home."

"Yes, far away," others agreed. "But where? Have they been in the court of the Tartar king all these years?"

In the meantime, the travellers, having washed and refreshed themselves with food and wine, began inquiring about the family. Who was still alive? And who had departed from this world? Who was living in Venice? And what members of the family had moved to other places? All these things they desired to know.

They were grieved to hear that, among others, the old grandparents were dead.

Later in the afternoon the servants were sent out with letters inviting the Polo relatives, old friends and some of the city nobles to a feast to be held that very night.

All afternoon the servants ran here and there. Extra help was brought into the kitchen. Special provisions were bought: wine, meats, game, sweets and other delicacies.

The tables were drawn together so that they made one long board that reached the full length of the dining hall. The chairs were placed close together to accommodate all who had been invited.

The Polos greeted their guests as they arrived. They were still dressed in their coarse and tattered travelling clothes. But after the first course had been served at the table, they cast these coarse garments to the floor and put on long robes of crimson satin. Later during the meal they changed to robes of damask and, finally, to robes of heavily embroidered scarlet velvet. And what was most surprising to those present was that after the Polos had removed their robes they carefully folded them and presented them to some of the guests.

"This," explained Marco, "is in strict accordance with Mongol custom. These robes were presented to us by Kublai Khan himself. But at present I had better say no more. Soon you will learn everything."

Those who heard his words looked at each other in bewilderment. It all seemed too fantastic to be true. Later, when the meal was over and the table cleared, Marco spoke.

"It is indeed difficult," admitted Marco, "to know where to begin. During our absence of twenty-four years, we have been in so many places and seen so many things that I hardly know what to speak of first. We have visited places where no man from Europe has ever been before. But most of the years that we were away, we lived in far-off Cathay in the court of the great emperor Kublai Khan, ruler of most of Asia."

He paused and looked about.

"I know it sounds unbelievable," he continued. "But I am telling the truth. We have been on a long journey, perhaps the longest that has ever been made. We have covered thousands of miles and now, after these many years, we are back. We are back from the wonderful Orient, back from the deserts of Persia, from Pamir and the lofty steppes of mysterious Tibet. We are back from Mongolia, Burma, Sumatra, Java; back from Ceylon and India; back from lands rich in marvels. We are returned from the dazzling court of Kublai Khan, who is richer and more powerful than all the kings of the world."

Then Marco went on to tell of many of the wonderful and curious things which they had seen in these distant lands. The guests listened politely but such fantastic things were hard to believe.

Nicolo and Maffeo could sense that Marco's words were being questioned. And so they picked up their old ragged travelling garments, which they previously had cast to the floor; then, taking knives, they ripped open the seams.

On the table before their guests they poured out diamonds, emeralds, pearls, rubies and other precious stones in great quantities. Never before had people in Venice seen so many large, valuable gems cast like pebbles before them.

Then Nicolo spoke. "Every word that Marco has just uttered is the truth. Where, then, would these gems come from?"

And Maffeo joined in. "It is the truth—and not a hundredth part of our adventures have you yet heard."

"In time, in time," said Marco, "you will hear everything. I have only outlined briefly where we have been and what we have been doing these long years. Now let us hear what has been happening at home."

One of the nobles of Venice rose and proposed that the Polos be elected to command one of the new war galleys. Then, turning to the three travellers, he explained.

"Our old enemy the Merchants Guild of Genoa has in recent years been raiding our merchant ships. They are more troublesome than the pirates of old. They are fighting bitterly for control of the Mediterranean trade. But this trade, as you know, has always been in the hands of our guild in Venice. Now, to protect our vessels and our trade lanes, we have built some war galleys, each manned by a hundred oars. And over each galley one of our great merchant houses will have command. Therefore, I propose to all now here assembled that one of the new galleys be commanded by the Polos."

"Yes." All voiced loud agreement.

But Maffeo said that he was weary from his long journey and begged to be excused. And Nicolo said that he expected to be away from Venice, in order to re-establish his business in various ports.

"Then Marco shall be the gentleman commander," insisted the nobleman.

"Yes. Let Marco command the galley!" some shouted.

"It is agreed," announced the nobleman. "One of the new galleys will be commanded by Marco of the Polo family."

Marco was proud of the great honour conferred upon him, little realizing at the time that the position of gentleman commander would one day bring him into great difficulty.

He remembered that during the years of his youth, those long years in which he waited for the return of his father and uncle, he often stood before the window of his room watching the trading vessels and the war galleys in the harbour. How many times have you seen the fast hundred-oar galleys race across the surface of the water. Then he was a boy. Now he was a man. And now he would have one of those war galleys under his command.

Later that night when the guests had gone home the travellers gathered up the jewels that were on the table. "Twenty-four years," said Nicolo. "How time has flown! It seems as though it were only yesterday that we sailed from home."

"And little did we know then," added Maffeo, "of all the marvels which we were to see."

"And the great Khan Kublai..." said Marco. "I wonder if he misses us as much as we miss him. He was good to us—and before we go to bed in our old home, let us drink a toast to his health."

They poured three glasses of rare wine and drank a toast to their good friend in far-off Cathay. They drank to his health, to his long life.

They drank this toast not knowing that two years before, while they were still on their long journey home, the great emperor Kublai had died.

This they did not know. Neither did they know the full extent of their good fortune in having left Cathay at the time they did. For with the death of the great Khan, the entire Orient was thrown into chaos. Many princes began warring for power. And the roads between Europe and the Orient were once more closed to all travellers. For hundreds of years to come, no one was again able to make the journey to Cathay. For only a brief period in history of the world had the road to Cathay been open. On this wonderful road the Polos had travelled. And no sooner had they returned home than the road was closed.

As for the Khan's pleasure city of Xanadu, Marco Polo was the last European ever to see it. For after the death of the Khan this beautiful garden city fell into desolate ruin. Weeds conquered the gardens. Neglect and time brought the pleasure palaces to dust and rubble.

The Polos drank another toast to the great Khan and to their safe return. Then they went to bed and slept once again under the roof of their old home in Venice. The year was 1295.

CHAPTER XXV

IN PRISON MARCO WROTE HIS TRUTHFUL BOOK

THREE YEARS LATER, in the month of September, a furious sea battle took place between the Genoese and Venetian war galleys.

The battle began early on a Sunday morning and lasted until dusk. While the Venetians had the wind in their favour, they also had the sun in their eyes. Nevertheless, they pressed forward with great daring and recklessness. Before noon they had captured ten Genoese galleys and made prisoners of the crews. One of these captured galleys they managed to man with their own Venetians and turn against the enemy. However, they were almost too wild in their pursuit and several of their galleys ran aground.

The Genoese, seeing this, took fresh courage and reorganized their forces. They formed into a single file and again went forward to engage the Venetians. In the battle that raged during most of that afternoon neither side could claim victory. Just as the sun was about to set, however, sixteen fresh Genoese galleys appeared unexpectedly. These sixteen galleys had become separated from the main flotilla the night before and had been considered lost. Now they suddenly appeared and fell on the Venetian flank with fresh force. This was the deciding blow. Against this additional force the Venetians were helpless.

Before darkness came, on this sad Sunday, the victory was complete. The Genoese had conquered.

The victors cut the proud banners of the vanquished Venetian galleys and allowed them to drag in the water. In this manner were the captives humiliated by the conquerors.

Then the captured galleys of the Venetians were rowed into the harbour of Genoa. And with these galleys came seven thousand prisoners. Among these prisoners was Marco Polo, Gentleman Commander.

The Genoese were cruel to their enemies. All prisoners, even those of highest rank, were put into chains. And many were starved to death or allowed to die from extreme neglect.

But the fame of Marco Polo was known in Genoa and he was treated with much consideration. He was placed in a cell with but one other prisoner, a scholarly gentleman named Rusticiano, from the city of Pisa. They soon became good friends.

Rusticiano, who had been in this prison for some time, knew some of the jailers and through them he managed to smuggle out a letter that Marco had written to his father. Nicolo Polo immediately appealed to the nobles of Venice to press for Marco's release. But the authorities of Genoa refused to surrender Marco. They said that all prisoners would have their freedom when the peace terms were finally agreed upon.

During all the long months while the peace negotiations were going on between the nobles of Venice and the authorities of Genoa, Marco amused his prison-mate Rusticiano with tales of the places and wonders he had seen in the far-off Orient.

And after each story Rusticiano would remark: "What a pity you do not write down all these things, otherwise it will be lost to the world. No man has ever seen such wonders!"

"Ah, that may be true," Marco would reply. "But who would believe me? If I recorded the truth I would only be branded a liar!"

"No matter. The truth in the end must win out over falsehood."

Every day Rusticiano urged Marco to write down his experiences. And finally one day Marco agreed to do so. He said it would help make the long hours in prison seem shorter. There was only one difficulty. He had travelled so far and seen so much that he could not possibly remember everything accurately and in its proper order. If only he had his notes—then he could easily reconstruct the entire journey.

"Where are your notes?" asked Rusticiano.

"I have them at home in Venice. They are precious to me. I brought them safely with me from Cathay. They are worth more to me than jewels."

Now Rusticiano wrote a letter to Marco's father and placed it, together with a gold piece, in the hands of one of the friendly jailers. Several weeks later this same jailer unlocked their cell door. He had a package for Rusticiano which he had smuggled into the prison. It contained Marco Polo's notes, pages and pages of thin paper filled with small handwriting.

"Now," said Rusticiano, "you can have no further excuses, especially as I am ready to serve as your scribe. I have parchment, ink and a quantity of goose quills. And all you have to do is to dictate and I will write it all down. When shall we begin?"

Rusticiano was eager to start. But Marco had first to study his notes and put everything in proper sequence. At length, one day he was ready.

His prison-mate sat with pen in hand. Marco had his notes spread out before him, and in a clear voice he began to dictate.

"Let us first write a prologue," said Marco, "and let it begin with these words: 'Ye Emperors, Kings, Dukes, Marquises, Earls, and Knights, and all other people desirous of knowing the diversities of the races of mankind, as well as the diversities of kingdoms, provinces, and regions of all parts of the East, read through this book, and ye will find in it the greatest and most marvellous characteristics of the peoples especially of Armenia, Persia, India, and Tartary, as they are severally related in the present work by Marco Polo, a wise and learned citizen of Venice, who states distinctly what things he saw and what things he heard from others. For this book will be a truthful one.'"

He spoke his words slowly and clearly. And the words he spoke Rusticiano wrote down. In this way and with these words began the record that has now become the most famous in all travel literature.

CHAPTER XXVI

A CENTURY LATER, CAME CHRISTOPHER COLUMBUS

When Marco Polo was finally released from prison, he and Rusticiano had finished recording his travel record. While writing this long work the prisoners had forgotten the grey prison walls. They imagined themselves in wonderful foreign lands, in the glittering court of Kublai Khan.

After Marco Polo returned to his home in Venice he managed to arrange for the prison release of his companion Rusticiano, who was happy to return to his home in Pisa. This friendship that began in prison was to endure for many years.

In time Marco Polo married a lady called Donata. She bore him three handsome daughters whom they named Fantina, Bellela and Moreta. And when his old father Nicolo and his uncle Maffeo died, Marco inherited all their cargo ships and warehouses. He became the head of the Polo family. He was now a very wealthy man and he used his wealth to help many of his relatives and less fortunate friends. And he became greatly respected and honoured in Venice.

The book of travels which he had dictated in prison quickly won fame. Many asked permission to read it and some even considered it so unique that they begged to be allowed to make copies. Several nobleman employed Scribes to make special copies on parchment, which they presented to kings and dukes. And so the name of Marco Polo became known throughout the entire breadth of Europe.

There was one thing, however, which grieved Marco greatly. There were some who refused to believe in the truth of this travel record. And they were bold enough to say that the entire thing was invented;

just one big lie from beginning to end. A million lies! They made fun of him and called him "Marco of the Millions". So persistent were these people in their attacks against him that the expression "Marco's Millions" has come down to us as meaning a lie. And to this day in Venice the courtyard of his old home is known as the "Court of the Millions".

Marco tried to defend himself against these attacks. "It is not a lie!" he would exclaim. "Every word is the truth!"

But he soon grew weary of it all and tried to avoid talking about his travels. These arguments seemed to him endless and of little use. Those who believed him, believed him with a full heart. And as for those who did not believe him, he knew that their minds were shut tightly and that he could never win them over.

Now it happened that when Marco Polo was seventy years old he fell ill. And there were some who, fearing he might die, came to his bedside and pleaded with him.

"Confess all!" they urged. "Confess that it has all been a hoax. Confess that it is all untrue before the breath leaves your body and it is too late."

"With my dying breath," said Marco, "I repeat that it is all true. Every word is the truth. I have not told even half of what I saw. But I told the truth, that I swear." These words he repeated over and over to his very last day.

When he died he was mourned by all the people of Venice. But there were few who understood the full worth of his accomplishment, nor the great influence his book was to have on the future world.

Over a hundred years after the death of Marco Polo a young man named Christopher Columbus, reading a copy of his travels, was greatly stirred. He was fired with a desire to find a short western water route to the lands described by Marco Polo. In time, this young man managed to set sail from Spain in quest of Marco Polo's Orient. But as we all know, he never reached these lands. Instead he discovered America.

- - - - - - - -

It is only in modern times that the full worth of Marco Polo's travels have been realized. Only now do we fully understand how indisputable is his claim to fame.

He was the very first traveller to trace a route across the entire length of Asia, naming and describing kingdom after kingdom. He was the first to record the deserts of Persia, the plateau of Pamir, the jade-bearing rivers of western China, the long Mongolian steppes from which sprung those Mongolian tribes that threatened to conquer the entire world. All these things, which were at that time unknown in Europe, he saw and recorded.

And it is through Marco Polo's eyes that we see an intimate picture of the brilliant court of Kublai Khan. His is the only known record of that famous pleasure city of Xanadu, the ruins of which were not discovered until centuries after his death. All this we owe to Marco Polo. All this and more.

He was the first traveller to reveal the vast wealth of China, its cultured cities, its great rivers, its rich manufactures, its commerce and its dense population. He was also the first to describe the Great Canal, paper money, those black stones which we now call coal, and hundreds of other things.

He was the very first to write of strange Tibet, of Burma with its golden towers, of Indo-China, of Japan with its pink pearls and its golden roofed palaces; the first to describe Java and cannibal Sumatra, Ceylon with its sacred tomb of Adam, and India; the first to describe Siberia and the Arctic regions where people rode in sledges drawn by dogs.

No other travel record contains so rich a store of marvels. No other traveller attempted so much and accomplished so much. All this rich catalogue of discoveries, the world owes to one man, Marco Polo.

Made in United States
Troutdale, OR
06/08/2024